CHR___ANS, JEWS and the END TIMES

God's Ultimate Plan For His people

RAY BACHMAN

Morning Star Ministries

Mountain Home, Arkansas

Copyright © 2014, 2016 by Ray Bachman

Second Edition published July 2016

Cover Photo: City Wall of Jerusalem, photograph by Jeanne Bachman, January, 2009.

Chapters One, Two, Three and Six are taken from other works by the author. Detailed documentation is included in the chapter notes.

ISBN: 978-1-4528-3741-3

Published by Morning Star Ministries, Mountain Home, Arkansas
Printed in the United States of America
For additional information go to www.morningstarmin.org
To contact the author: bachmanjr@gmail.com
To order this book: www.createspace.com/3450322

Dedicated
To All Who Are
Children of Abraham
By Faith in Messiah
Both Jew and Gentile

Also by Ray Bachman

BIBLE PROPHECY

The Love Letters of Jesus
The God Who Remembers

BIBLE STUDY

Eight Secrets to Spiritual Healing
Drastic Discipleship
Fitly Joined Together
Twelve Hours to Decide

INSPIRATION AND DEVOTIONAL

The King and I
The 3:16's
Looking Up! Everyday
God Cares

Table of Contents

Preface

What is it that Christians don't know about the Jews? The answer in many cases would be, "Almost everything!" I say that, not with an accusatory tone, but out of reflection on my own experience. As I began to study more and more of Bible prophecy, I began to realize that there was more and more of the Jewish background of the Scriptures which I did not possess.

That was not only frustrating, but, in a real sense, rather maddening, since I have been a Christian most of my life and had spent over forty years in the ministry as a preacher and teacher of the Bible.

It is most amazing how the Scriptures begin to take on fresh light and more profound insight when we study the Bible with an increasing emphasis on our Jewish roots rather than wrapping everything we read in a narrow, limited Christian perspective.

We are Christians, but not just New Testament ones. We are Christians whose very roots are deeply imbedded in the Old Testament. To grasp the historical and spiritual realities which undergird our faith enables us to see the Scriptures in a clearer light. This is especially true in the area of Bible prophecy.

This book is not a unified treatise on the subject of the relationship of Jewish roots to Christian doctrine. Rather, it is a series of studies on topics that will cover that relationship, but with no attempt at being a scholarly undertaking of a very broad subject. Some of the articles are from previously published materials, others are seen here for the first time.

I have spent the greater part of my ministry as a pastor. I write, therefore, as I preach and teach. That is, with a desire to put in the hands of my flock a useable and understandable work that can assist God's people in the pew and classroom in comprehending His plan, His purpose and His procedures for all of His people, whether Jew or Gentile.

To that end, I present this work as a practical tool for those like myself who find themselves lacking in the fundamentals of knowing how God is bringing His ultimate plan to completion for His people. As we rapidly approach the end of this age when we see Yeshua, the Messiah, once again taking center stage of life on this earth, this understanding will assist us to be prepared for the wonderful things which God has planned. May these writings be a blessing to you.

Study One

The Jews and Bible Prophecy[1]

Read Genesis 12:1-7

As Christians we may well ask ourselves why we would want to embark upon a study about the relationship of Christians and Jews in the End Times. Many of us have had no guidance in this area of Biblical study. In fact, we have had an unconscious training in the opposite direction—God is done with the Jews and all of His future plans relate to the Church of Jesus.

Unfortunately, much of this kind of thinking has been promulgated without consulting God about His opinion. We need to focus on some powerful Scripture verses that clearly state that God has yet a great plan for the people whom He chose to be His unique people in this world. What does He say about their future?

I will bring them out from the nations and gather them from the countries, and I will bring them into their own land. I will pasture them on the mountains of Israel, in the ravines and in all the settlements in the land. I will tend them in a good pasture, and the mountain heights of Israel will be their grazing land. There they will lie down in good grazing land, and there they will feed in a rich pasture on the mountains of Israel. I myself will tend my sheep and have them lie down, declares the sovereign Lord (Ezekiel 34:13f).

On that day a fountain will be opened to the house of David and the inhabitants of Jerusalem, to cleanse them from sin and impurity. . . .They will call on my name and I will answer them; I will say, "They are my people," and they will say, "The Lord is our God" (Zechariah 13:1, 9b).

" 'For I will take you out of the nations; I will gather you from all the countries and bring you back into your own land. I will sprinkle clean water on you, and you will be clean; I will cleanse you from all your impurities and from all your idols. I will give you a new heart and put a new spirit in you; I will remove from you your heart of stone and give you a heart of flesh. And I will put my Spirit in you and move you to follow my decrees and be careful to keep my laws. You will live in the land I gave your forefathers; you will be my people, and I will be your God.' " (Ezekiel 36:24-28).

Thus, we have clear statements of the message that the prophets received from the Lord. It is a message to the Hebrews or Jews and it foretells that in the End Times the surviving remnant of the Jews will turn to Jesus Christ, whom they will know as *Yeshua ha Mashiach*, Jesus the Messiah.

Of course the message, while directed to the Jews, has world-wide implications. It will impact the Church of Jesus because of its relationship to Israel. It will drastically affect virtually all of the political nations of the entire world as they will be involved in the last dramatic battle known as Armageddon. Unfortunately, many in the Church today, along with the general population, have little understanding of Bible prophecy. This is nothing less than a major theological disaster! In great measure, the Church has been ripped from its roots in Judaism. Thus, we don't understand God's plan for the Jews, our ability to properly interpret Scripture is severely handicapped and the interpretation of Bible prophecy is often incorrect or is ignored to a level of near totality.

As we prepare to scrutinize the relationship of Christians and Jews in the End Times, we will lay some foundational underpinning for our study. If we want to really understand what God is sharing through the prophets' words, we will be greatly aided if we first of all examine, in at least a cursory fashion, how God has dealt with the Jews in times past. If we keep in mind that everything God was saying through the Old Testament prophets was rooted and grounded in an understanding of God's relationship with His chosen people, the Jews, then our comprehension will be greatly enhanced and much more likely to be correct.

Much of what we say in this chapter will not be new to the majority of you. However, it may help to put in a logical arrangement many of the things we know in a rather piecemeal fashion and without connecting the dots as to how it all fits together. If we look carefully at God's dealing with the Jews in the past, we shall be enabled to discern His plan for them for the future, and thus, have a fuller comprehension of how Christians also fit into His future plans. All of His future designs for man are intimately tied together, and like it or not, they all revolve around His people Israel. John Walvoord, one of the leading scholars of Bible prophecy of the last century, has well summarized this truth.

For a Gentile Christian, the subject of Israel in prophecy does not immediately have an appeal as an important doctrine. When one begins to study prophecy in the Bible, however, it soon becomes evident that Israel is in the center of biblical prophecy and that to understand prophecy as a whole one must understand God's purpose for Israel.[2]

This first study, therefore, is to give ourselves a brief overview of Jewish history that will enable us to more fully comprehend the background against which the prophets' communications are delivered. The messages the prophets were given from God were not unique to themselves, but are consistent with other prophetic messages throughout the entire Bible. None of them stand alone, but rather each finds its fullness of meaning in the context of Jewish history, both past and future.

This will all be much clearer if we take time to consider the Jewish historical roots before we dig too deeply into the marvelous End Times treasures which await in both testaments. There is indeed a great connection between believers in Jesus, the Christ, and those whom God has called to know and serve through their Messiah, *Yeshua.*

What Do We Know of the Jews?

For most Gentiles (for our purposes that includes all non-Jews) the knowledge possessed of Jews, Judaism and the nation of Israel is woefully inadequate. This is true, unfortunately, for both Christians and non-believers alike. There are a number of reasons for this. In my own case, for instance, I grew up in a small Midwestern town where, as far as I know, we had not a single Jewish resident.

My church was one of that vast multitude of denominations which subscribe to that most unbiblical doctrine of Replacement Theology which says that God is finished with the Jews because of their rejection of Jesus at His first Advent and therefore they have no future as far as God is concerned.

In my Army experience and in my college and university days I had little or no contact or teaching about the Jewish people. In short, I neither knew Jews nor about Jews. I suppose the one idea I picked up from off-the-cuff remarks was that all Jews were rich and that in some obscure way they controlled the entire world.

However, like a lot of persons, I did know something of the Jews. Since I grew up in the church, I had been taught a lot of Old Testament Jewish stories. Joseph and his many-colored coat was a favorite as were the tales of Daniel in the Lion's Den and the three Hebrew children in the fiery furnace. Crossing the Red Sea on dry ground in the Exodus was a most exciting tale. There were many others as well, but there was a downside to those stories.

These exciting tales were wonderfully positive examples of faith in God and experiencing His deliverance or help. That's great! But there is more. These lessons are seldom taught in the context of Jewish history. So, while we know some great examples from Jewish history, most of us know little of Jewish history. That has made a lot of our Bible study anemic and often leading to improper conclusions. But, at least we do know a little something of the Jews.

Another area of knowledge may be one which we unwittingly possess. That is, the Jews today are not all in one area, often called the Holy Land, as they were in Bible days. Now, we see them scattered throughout the world. There is a special word to describe this wide distribution; it is known as the Dispersion, or the Diaspora.

This fleeing to the far ends of the earth began after the Romans attacked Israel and Jerusalem, completely destroying the Jewish Temple in A.D. 70. It was only in the last century that the Jews began to immigrate back to the national homeland in large numbers.

The return to the land, or *aliya*, brings us to a third something we know of the Jews. Not only are they in their land today, but they are there as a nation. One of the most significant days in all of history took place on May 14, 1948, when Israel declared itself a nation. That one event set in place for the first time in history the condition for many of the end times prophecies to begin to be fulfilled

Today, Israel dominates world headlines. Every other nation, especially in the Middle East is surveyed in relation to the nation of Israel. Never has there been a day when the daily news and the Word of God can be so fully harmonized. We are living in a day of rapid fulfillment of prophecy, and the exciting Biblical message is indeed one which we desperately need to study, to understand and to take appropriate action in light of its pronouncements.

So, while we do know some things about the Jews, there are often some very important things we do not know about these people who are called "God's Chosen People" Often, we do not have even the slightest idea of why they are termed as chosen. More often than not we are prone to believe it has something to do with being chosen because they were so good. On the contrary, when they had no goodness to commend them, God simply selected them and set them apart to be a people uniquely used of Himself to convey his message of love and grace to the entire world. Upon receiving his call to leave his homeland and go to a place to which God would direct, Abram received this promise from God, "all peoples on earth will be blessed through you" (Genesis 12:3).

As we consider the study of Bible prophecy, we will find ourselves coming up short in our understanding if we do not know the plan God has for Jews in End Times events. While we are rather naturally prone to look at how prophecy might affect us as Christians, or even as unbelievers in the world, God has a different viewpoint. He looks at the coming events in prophecy in light of the Jews and His covenants with them which God remembers forever. We would do well to begin to learn to see as God sees when we study his holy Word.

A second important factor we may fail to comprehend is the relationship of the nation of Israel and prophecy. Israel is not just a nation like any other. It is a nation which has profound significance in all that will take place in the End Times, and it is all closely related to their history. As we study what the Scriptures say about forthcoming events, we will find that we need to study with our eyes and ears attuned to what is taking place in the tiny little nation at the eastern end of the Mediterranean It may be small but with an importance that far outweighs the common perception.

A Brief History of the Jews

When we study history we are accustomed to looking at it as a long straight line of dates and events. And, indeed, that is what history is. However, the study can become quite boring and often very difficult to keep all those dates, names and places in order. When we look at Jewish history, we are in luck; there is an easier way. We can more easily get a grasp on Jewish life and history when we think of it not as a straight line but as a series of cycles upon that line.

The Jewish people are uniquely related to the land. Later in the chapter we will consider the Land Covenant which God made with the Jews. While the cycles we want to consider are normally related to a most significant person and a noteworthy event, they are, unlike the history of other nations, having to do with whether the Jews are in their land or not. The cycles, as we will see, begin and end with the people being either in their land or out of their land.

As a beginning point we need to remind ourselves that in the beginning there were no Jews. Adam and Eve were not Jews. In creation there were just regular, ordinary people like us. However, those folks who were our earliest ancestors quickly got into serious trouble because of their disobedience. This is what is usually known as the Fall, the willful descent from the wonderful position for which mankind had been created. This inherent sinfulness known as Original Sin was passed on to all the descendents of Adam.

But God wanted to restore man so He came up with a plan. That plan was to chose a people through whom He could put man back into right relationship with Himself. That people began, with God's call to Abraham, to follow and serve God. Thus, the Chosen People were only special in the calling and responsibility which God gave them. With that brief background, let us now take a quick look at this cyclical history of these special people.

To enable us to grasp this unique aspect of Jewish story, we will use a series of drawings which will give us a visible picture of this unusual phenomenon. Figure 1 shows how the beginning and end of each cycle is related to a predominate individual. Their names are shown near the top of the drawing. There is often also a dramatic event associated with each cycle. These are shown below the central time line, i.e., the Exodus. The light colored semi-circles

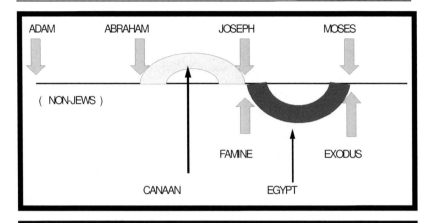

Figure 1. Timeline showing the beginning of the Jews beginning with Abraham through Moses. Chart is not to time scale.

above the timeline represent a period of time when the Hebrews were by and large dwelling in their own land while the dark semi-circles below the timeline indicates that the people were dwelling predominately outside their land. The names of locations of their dwelling place are near the bottom of the drawing.

Thus, we see that in the beginning from Adam to Abraham, there were no Jews. When God called Abraham, He instructed him to take his family and go to a land that God would show him. The ordinary name for that land is Canaan and is the primary place that Abraham and his descendents resided until forced to go to Egypt because of great famine in Canaan. The outstanding human instrument in that move was Joseph. For 400 years the rapidly growing family of Abraham's off spring was in Egypt until they left under the leadership of Moses. That concludes the first in-the-land, out-of-the-land cycle. We note something unique, however, when we come to the next cycle.

When the Hebrews crossed the Red Sea and left Egypt behind, we would expect the next half circle to be above the line indicating that they were back in their own land once again. However, we know from history that would be making an incorrect assumption. They had themselves thought they would soon be back in the land of milk and honey. But it was not to be so. They would spend the next 40 years in the desert wilderness. Thus, on our timeline as we see in Figure 2, we have two consecutive loops indicating they were out of the land. This is unique and only happened that once. Moses was not only the one who led them out of captivity, but remained their leader until time for them to return to their land.

Then it was Joshua who led them back into the land of promise across the Jordan and into the conquest of the land that was really theirs but now inhabited by others. Sounds a bit like a foretaste of current events, does it not? So the Jews were back home and would be there for quite a long time. However, due to their unfaithfulness to the Lord, the Jews were again destined to leave for foreign territory.

God allowed the Babylonian King Nebuchadnezzar to be used as an instrument of His judgment. Over a period of years this foreign king repeatedly raided the country of the Israelites, taking the people back to Babylon as captives and totally destroying Jerusalem and the beautiful Temple which stood there. It is from this period that we learned some of our Sunday School stories: i.e., Daniel, Meshach, Shadrack and Abednego.

This captivity came to an end seventy years later, exactly as foretold in Bible prophecy, when the new King of Babylon, Cyrus, allowed the people to return to their land. He instructed them to rebuild the Temple when they got back to Jerusalem. Zerubbabel

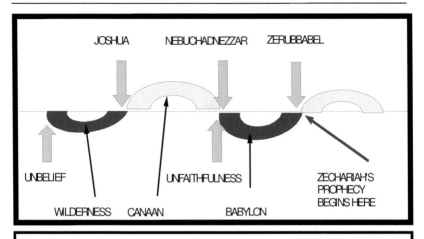

Figure 2. Hebrew timeline from entering the wilderness until the time of residing in the land after returning from the exile in Babylon.

was the leader of the nation and was the one who was to supervise the Temple rebuilding.

In a real sense, that is all the history we need to help us know the background from which the exiles returned and were functioning once again in the land which God gave them. But we dare not end our timeline there, for several of the prophets spell out for us that there are two more cycles to take place. The exciting aspect of this is that these final two cycles are those which we are being privileged to be part of in these present days.

We far too often make one of two diametrically opposed errors in our conception of the prophetic Biblical message: we think either that prophecy is all far past and not very interesting or it is so far in the future that we really need not be concerned about it. But, how exciting it is to be living in days that we can see prophecy coming to pass and indeed taking place in our own time. This has always been true to an extent, but the present days are filled with events so precisely fitting into God's prophetic time table that it is difficult to ignore them. The big question for us really is seeing how these events are all tied together and are dramatically moving toward a final destiny.

As we came to the end of Figure 2, we said that after the Jews were back in their homeland and had completed the rebuilding of the Temple, that they dwelt in the land until the destruction of Jerusalem by Titus. We see that event noted at the beginning of Figure 3. That scattering which began then continued for over 1800 years. The dark semi-circle in Figure 3 representing that dispersion should, of course, be much longer. That period which began in A.D. 70 has continued until today. But near the end of the 19th century, the Jewish people began to come back to the land out of the Diaspora.

The next high point on our chart is the birth of the nation of Israel on May 14, 1948. It is at that point that we are once again showing the Jewish people in their land. But that is somewhat misleading, as about one-half of all the Jews in the world are still not in Israel. But the return is continuing at a fast pace. This continual flow of Jews back to the land is a contemporary fulfillment of what God spoke in Amos 9:14f:

> *"I will bring back my exiled people Israel; they will rebuild the ruined cities and live in them. They will plant vineyards and drink their wine; they will make gardens and eat their fruit. I will plant Israel in their own land, never again to be uprooted from the land I have given them,"* says the Lord your God.

So that places us presently somewhere in the center of the timeline in Figure 3. While not all of the Jews are in the land, they do

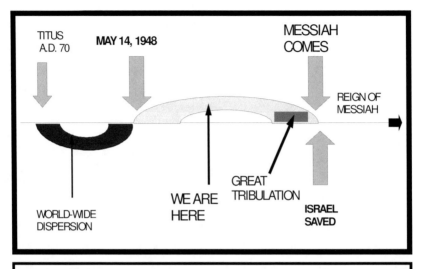

Figure 3. From the dispersion of Israel following the fall of Rome in A.D. 70 to the Millennial Reign of Messiah. The present day is located on this portion of the timeline.

have a nation in the land promised to them, so we are considering them to once again be in the land. As you see, it is in the time of this restoration to the land that we currently reside. While we do not know exactly where we are in the time line, we do know that this present time of Israel's sojourn in the land, which God says through Amos and other prophets will be a permanent one, will include near its end a seven year period of Tribulation. Then Jesus will come and the Jewish people will turn to Him *en masse* and accept Him as their long-awaited Messiah. Following that, Yeshua will establish His 1,000 year reign over the earth with Jerusalem as its capital ..

This cyclical nature of the Jewish people residing either in or out of the land given them by God has profound implications for our understanding of all Bible prophecy. We can't know and understand the role of the Jews in the End Times if we don't know about the Jews in the beginning. This brief look at their history will be of help as we delve into the prophecies which God has given. However, we now turn to an even more important part of Jewish history that plays a most significant function as we watch for End Times prophecy to play out.

God's Blessing Covenant with the Jews

The Jewish people began with a call from God to Abram (later renamed Abraham) to become a unique people who would carry out a most important plan that God had for the world. He chose them for a very specific purpose. We find this calling spelled out in Genesis 12:1-3, and every follower of God , whether Jew or Gentile, needs to know and understand this calling if we really want to know what God's plan has been, is and will be for the Jewish people and how this relates to the entirety of the world.

The Lord had said to Abram, "Leave your country, your people and your father's household and go to the land I will show you. I will make you into a great nation and I will bless you; I will make your name great, and you will be a blessing. I will bless those who bless you, and whoever curses you I will curse; and all peoples on earth will be blessed through you" (Genesis 12:1-3)

Thus, the Jews, though not yet called by that name, began with God's call to Abraham and the seven promises He gave them. This is often quite appropriately called the Abrahamic Covenant. That title, however, may subtly lead us to confirm the error of many who claim that this covenant was only for Abraham and not also to his descendents forever. Whether the covenants which God made with the Jews were only temporary contracts, which were negated by the disobedience and unfaithfulness of the Jews, or a permanent covenant which remains intact forever because the words are based on the permanence of the promises of God is the issue at stake here. And this issue is of utmost importance in the contemporary world setting.

I like to call this the **Covenant of Blessing** because it consists of seven irreversible statements by God that have profound importance in all of Bible prophecy. The first promise is that God would make Abraham and his descendents into a great nation. That has been true in the past, they are a most important nation today, and they will have even greater impact in the future.

Secondly, God promises that Abraham's family will be blessed by God. Even a casual reading of the Old Testament will reveal the truth of that promise and should cause us to expect that His blessing will continue to reside on these people.

A third promised blessing is that Abraham, and by implication all those who follow, will have a name made great by God. After a while these chosen ones where called Hebrews, then Jews, and later by the name of Israel which will be their name forever. When we come to the fourth promised blessing, it has to do with their responsibility. They will not only be a people blessed by God but He will make them to be a blessing to the other peoples of the earth. In God's mind it is not only a wonderful thing to be blessed, it is a blessing to be a blessing to others.

The fifth and sixth promises are the front and back sides of the same thing. The front side is that God will not only bless Abraham's descendents but He will also bless those who bless the Jews.

On the flip side, He promises that whoever curses the followers of Abraham will in return know the curse of God. God is so intent on having his Chosen People be blessed that He has recruited the entire population of the world to assist Him in doing so. Again, this is a promise that has overwhelming importance as we see our world today choosing up sides, and most are aligning themselves against the descendents of Abraham. This antagonism we know as anti-Semitism.

The final of the seven blessings has a close relationship with the fourth. It actually spells out just whom are to be the recipients of the blessings of these special people. God says that all peoples on earth will be blessed through them.

Verses two and three of Genesis twelve are some of the most potent verses in the entire Bible. They set in motion a plan that God will see fulfilled, no matter how many times it appears that the covenant is null and void. Since God's covenants depend on His supreme will, not on man's performance, we can with confidence know that they will all be completed in God's timing. These seven promises of the Covenant of Blessing are all in various stages of fulfillment either having been fulfilled, are presently being fulfilled or are to be fulfilled in the future.

Lest anyone should doubt whether the Jews will survive to the end and know the fruition of all that God has promised, He has made a strong statement about the longevity of the Jewish people. This counters the present-day claims and actions of those whose aim is to eliminate the Jews forever. He spoke through another of His prophets and proclaimed,

". . .he who appoints the sun to shine by day, who decrees the moon and stars to shine by night, who stirs up the sea so that its waves roar—the Lord Almighty is his name. Only if these decrees vanish from my sight," declares the Lord, "will the descendents of Israel ever cease to be a nation before me" (Jeremiah 31:35F).

God's Land Covenant with the Jews

The second covenant is what we might call the **Land Covenant**. This set of promises from God was made over a period of time, to several different persons, and at a variety of locales. We will not take time to deeply analyze each aspect of this covenant, but it is necessary to emphasize how critical this covenant is because it is at the root of much of the dissension in our world today over the relationship of Israel to other nations.

One of this generation's most gifted teachers of Bible prophecy, Hal Lindsey, has succinctly voiced this conflict.

The creation of a special people with unconditional promises of an everlasting title deed to specific land in the Middle East has brought unique problems to this world.[3]

The first installment of the Land Covenant began in the same place and at the same time as the Covenant of Blessing, but it was enlarged and more fully delineated at later times. Before spelling out the blessings which Abram and his descendents would enjoy, God, as an integral part of the call, told Abram that he should leave his own country and go to the land that he would be shown. Thus, Abraham was not only to enjoy God's blessings, but he was to do so in a place, a specific land, that God would show him. We know,

25

from the Old Testament story of his journey, that place was called Canaan because it was occupied by the Canaanites.

After Abraham and his family arrived in Canaan, they came to Shechem. There God made it clear that the title deed to the land was not only to Abraham, but to his descendents. God spoke very clearly in words that need no interpretation. "To your offspring I will give this land" (Genesis 12:7). This indicates that the land was a continuing gift that spans all generations from Abraham onward.

God was not yet done with his covenant, however. After Abraham and Lot had parted company (Genesis 13), Abraham was living in Canaan and he heard God giving even more detail about the land.

> *Lift up your eyes from where you are and look north and south, east and west. All the land that you see I will give to you and your offspring forever. . . .Go, walk through the length and breadth of the land, for I am giving it to you* (Genesis 13:14, 15, 17).

The highly important new facet that was received at Shechem was the unqualified statement that the land gift was a "forever" gift. It could never be rescinded. Though Israel might be not occupying the land, as we saw earlier in the chapter, the land forever belongs to the descendents of Abraham. That very fact is at the heart and soul of all the present-day conflict between Israel and the Palestinians over rights to the Gaza Strip, so-called West Bank, East Jerusalem and the Temple Mount. There will never be a permanent settlement to this issue until Jesus the Messiah comes in power and great glory and takes everlasting control of the land.

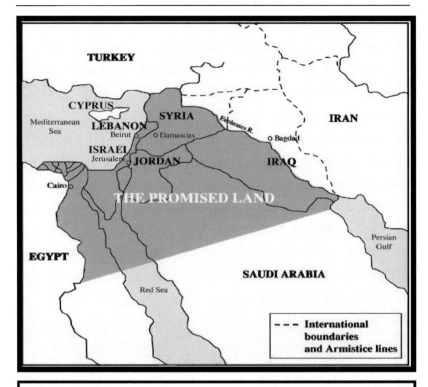

Figure 4. The darkest shaded area may show the great amount of land promised to Israel by God. Only a small fraction is presently occupied by the nation.

There are yet at least two more instances of God confirming the Land Covenant. Abraham settled in Mamre, near Hebron. Again, God came and further delineated the boundaries of the land that was being given to the Hebrew people. This is a very clear-cut setting forth of just what extent of land God was designating as a permanent possession of His Chosen People.

On that day the Lord made a covenant with Abram and said, "To your descendents I give this land, from the river

27

of Egypt to the great river, the Euphrates—the land of the Kenites, Kenizzites, Kadmonites, Hittites, Perizzites, Rehaites, Amorites, Canaanites, Girgashites and Jebusites (Genesis 15:18-21).

We will not take time to analyze all the different peoples who were occupying the land at this time. It is imperative, however, that we examine the extent of the boundaries of which God speaks. The people groups named by God were living in that areas that today comprise Lebanon, Syria, much of Jordan as well as Israel.

Figure 4 enables us to gain an appreciation for the vastness of the territory involved. The river of Egypt is most likely the Nile, although some claim it to be a river further east. The Euphrates has its headwaters far north of Lebanon in present-day Turkey and angles south and east to join with the Tigris River shortly before entering the Persian Gulf. Its total length is about 2,235 miles. Because we have not carefully studied the Holy Scriptures, we can easily think that any promise God made concerning a Land Covenant, only refers to the small territory presently occupied by Israel and the Jewish people.

But there is yet one more part of the covenant we need to know. Joshua, the successor of Moses when the people entered the land of promise after the wilderness wandering, reported that God had spoken through Moses and given yet another strong word about the land. "So on that day Moses swore to me, "The land on which your feet have walked will be your inheritance and that of your children forever, because you have followed the Lord my God wholeheartedly" (Joshua 14:9). Since Joshua had been in the land of Goshen in Egypt and then the entire wilderness wanderings, the land promised in this instance would include Goshen, (which lies east of the Nile) and all of the Sinai Peninsula where his feet trod for forty years.

Can we really believe that the promises made by God so long ago still are relevant and binding today. Many in our world think not. But what we think with our finite minds does not matter. What does God's Word say?

This distinct family line through which God's covenant promises were to be fulfilled is affirmed later in the Bible. For example, in Psalm 105:8-11, we read, "He remembers his covenants forever, the word he commanded, for a thousand generations, the covenant he made with Abraham, the oath he swore to Isaac. He confirmed it to Jacob, as a decree, to Israel as an everlasting covenant: 'To you I will give the land of Canaan as the portion you will inherit.'"

Clearly, the land promises made by God and recorded in the bible are for the descendents of Abraham, Isaac, and Jacob—the Jews. From a biblical perspective, there is virtually no question about God's intended recipients of the land.[4]

So we see that God has allotted a giant portion of land for the Jewish people. They have never occupied most of it. The place we call Israel today is only a miniscule portion of what God has said should be theirs. The prophetic writers quote God as saying His people must be back in the land living as a nation before the development of the End Times scenario. Keep watching land developments in the Middle East. They are sure to have dramatic implications for the future of Israel and the rest of the world, as well. Elwood McQuaid well summarizes the Land Covenant.

What we learn from these foundational passages is that land rights for Israel are, from a biblical viewpoint, nonnegotiable. Whether the Jewish people are in or out of their land at any particular juncture in history is irrelevant. Eretz Israel belongs to the Jewish people. [5]

God's Lineage Covenant With the Jews

Having surveyed the Covenant of Blessing and the Land Covenant, we now come to a third and even more important promise of God to the Hebrews, that of the **Lineage Covenant** or the Davidic Covenant as it is often called. This covenant is key because all the promises of God to Israel are irrelevant without a Messiah. God had planned ahead from before the foundation of the world that from these people whom He would call and bless would come a Messiah, or anointed One, to be the salvation of all people.

So, from Abraham onward God had a plan in place that would insure the proper persons in each generation would fulfill their appointed role so that ultimately there would appear the Messiah in exactly the proper time and with the precise ancestry that God required. He left nothing to chance in this regard. There were many opportunities for this critical lineage to get off track, but through God's intervention, it was marvelously fulfilled.

The names and stories involved in this lineage are indeed interesting. Matthew, in the first chapter of his gospel account, provides a compilation of the fourteen generations from Abraham to Jesus, tracing the record from the standpoint of Joseph, who served as the earthly father of Jesus the Messiah. Luke's genealogy in chapter three of His gospel is considerably different and presents a most interesting study of names and people. His main emphasis is on the blood line of Mary, the mother of Jesus. While we have not the time nor space to discuss these lists of Jesus' ancestors, one thing is clear: He came in precise fulfillment of God's plan of redemption. We note as a matter of interest this matter of God's keeping the lineage intact. The Messiah would come from Abraham through Isaac, not by way of Ishmael the elder son by Sara's handmaiden. Then the line would go from Isaac through Jacob rather than Esau, the firstborn of the twin sons of Isaac. From Jacob, the line is traced to David and from him to *Yeshua ha Mashiach*, Jesus the Messiah. When you read the stories of these Old Testament heroes, keep in mind how their lives related to the lineage of the Messiah.

God emphasized the primacy of the correct lineage by reiterating aspects of the covenants as the flow of life moved onward. To Abraham He said, "But my covenant I will establish with Isaac, whom Sarah will bear to you by this time next year" (Genesis 17:21). Then to Jacob, in the next succeeding generation, He promised, "I will give you and your descendents the land, your descendents will be like the dust of the earth, all people on earth will be blessed through you" (Genesis 28:13-14).

King David plays a very critical role in this entire scenario. God's promise to him was extensive, but we extract a few sentences to uphold the idea of God's intense interest in the lineage of the Messiah. God instructed Nathan the prophet to tell David,

> "'The Lord declares to you that the Lord himself will establish a house for you. . .I will raise up your offspring to succeed you. . .I will establish the throne of his kingdom forever. . .Your house and your kingdom will endure forever before me; your throne will be established forever'" (2 Samuel 7:11-16).

The Hebrews, or Jews, began with Abraham and their history is moving toward only one thing—one spectacular event—the day when Messiah Jesus, or Yeshua in Hebrew, is Israel's Priest and their King and their Savior. Notice, that the reference is to a specific offspring of David, as Samuel refers to *his* kingdom. Thus, God gave the Davidic Covenant because One from the line of David would ultimately sit upon David's throne as the Messiah. The Psalmist affirms the certainty of God's fulfilling His covenants:

> *He remembers his covenants forever, the word he commanded, for a thousand generations, the covenant he made with Abraham, the oath he swore to Isaac. He confirmed it to Jacob as a decree, to Israel as an everlasting covenant* (Psalm 105:8-10).

God's New Covenant with the Jews

So we have seen to this point that God has made three unbreakable and everlasting covenants with Abraham and his descendents. There is the Blessing Covenant or Abrahamic Covenant, there is the Land Covenant, made to Abraham and repeated and enlarged upon to others. Thirdly, there is the Lineage Covenant, or Davidic Covenant, in which God promised a Messiah to come from the seed of Abraham in a very specific lineage. But, that is not the end! God has yet another promise to the people known as the Jews.

This final and ultimate covenant is the **New Covenant** in Christ Jesus. This is sometimes difficult for both Jews and the Church of Jesus to understand. Far too often we fail to recognize the deep connection between Christianity and Judaism. Jews are often fearful of believing anything having to do with Christianity could be in their future. Christians are reluctant to see how the Jews and their system of rituals and sacrifices can in any way come to salvation.

We must trust the sacred Scriptures enough to believe that there can be no contradiction between the two Testaments. We must believe enough in the saving grace of God to know that whether we fully understand it all or not, the Jews must be saved the same way as every other person—by trusting in the Lord Jesus and calling unto Him for salvation. Peter was fully comprehending this truth when he preached on the day of Pentecost. He was speaking primarily to a Jewish audience which asked him how they could be saved. His unequivocal reply was, "Repent and be baptized, every one of you, in the name of Jesus Christ for the forgiveness of sins" (Acts 2:38).

A few days later he was brought before the Jewish Sanhedrin and was quizzed about the things the apostles were doing in the name of Jesus. To make clear, for everyone, Peter spoke those potent words that delineated for all time the singular way to know God. "Salvation is found in no one else, for there is no other name under heaven given to men by which we must be saved" (Acts 4:12).

So we find that in this new covenant, Jews are saved only by looking to Jesus. We are often unaware of the fact that Jews have been, are being and will be saved only through faith in *Yeshua ha Mashiach*. As testimony to this truth, there are today more than 150 Messianic Jewish congregations in Israel who believe in and worship Jesus as their Messiah.

Another sticking point for many Christians is Paul's statement, "And so all Israel will be saved" (Romans 11:26). This does not mean all the Jews who have lived over all time. Rather, it is a reference to the remnant of the Jews who survive the Great Tribulation. Zechariah tells us the exciting prophecy of how they will look upon Jesus and be pierced in their heart and cry out to Him for salvation. This will take place when He returns in power and great glory at the conclusion of the Tribulation period.

So what does this all mean for the relationship of believers in Christ as they assess their relationship to Jews today? McQuaid has some powerful statements for us to consider.

> *In other words, what has been given to us through Jewry is not a marginal asset; it comprises the core of the faith we possess, an essence of the indispensable aspects of our spiritual heritage.*
>
> *Could God have chosen to do things another way? Most certainly. But He didn't. He brought into the world a Chosen People, thoroughly human—ordinary, if you will— but through them He chose to do extraordinary things, and we are all beneficiaries of the marvel that is the Jew.*
>
> *It is striking indeed to see that every anti-Semitic group or movement attempts to separate Christ from His Jewish origins.*[6]

Having said all this about the history and purpose of the Jews, what must happen for Israel to fulfill God's plan and purpose? It seems there are four things needed for this to take place.

1. The Jews must be regathered from their world-wide dispersion. This is happening today on a large scale with about half of all Jews in the world now living in the nation of Israel.
2. They must be living as a nation in their own land. This is a reality. Israel again became a nation on May 14, 1948, and

is now one of the leading nations of the world.

3. The people must be living in a faith relationship with their Messiah. Today the people are being restored to the land. The day is rapidly approaching when the Jews will be restored to the Lord.

4. They must be fulfilling the calling of God to be a blessing to the nations of the world. After the return of Jesus and the salvation of the Jews, they will indeed fill that exciting role.

A climactic verse in Zechariah's prophecy says, "On that day a fountain will be opened to the house of David and the inhabitants of Jerusalem, to cleanse them from sin and impurity" (13:1). That fountain, of course, is the fountain of the blood of Calvary that cleanses from sin and the unrighteousness of the heart. How very similar is this Old Testament prophetic verse to a statement made by John in the New Testament, "If we confess our sins, he is faithful and just to forgive us our sins and purify us from all unrighteousness" (I John 1:9).

Why Support Israel?

After having read this chapter, you may well feel you have a better understanding of Jewish history and God's plan for these people whom He has chosen for a very unique role for all mankind. But, this new understanding may have led you to questions you have hitherto never confronted in your thinking. The position of this book is that we must draw closer to Israel as a nation and to the Jews as a people. In what specific ways should we respond?

John Hagee, a pastor who strongly supports the Jewish people and heads an organization called Christians United for Israel, CUFI, has given us five powerful reasons for Christians to stand with Israel.

1. Israel is the only nation created by a sovereign act of God. Israel belongs to God Himself! As Creator of heaven and earth (Gen. 1:1), God had the right of ownership to give the land to whomever He chose. Therefore, modern-day Palestinians have no biblical mandate to own the land

2. Christians owe a debt of eternal gratitude to the Jewish people for their contributions, which gave birth to the Christian faith. Paul recorded in Romans 15:27, "For if the Gentiles have been partakers of their [the Jews] spiritual things, their duty is also to minister to them in material thing." Consider what the Jewish people have given to Christianity:The sacred Scripture, the prophets, the patriarchs, Mary, Joseph and Jesus of Nazareth, the twelve disciples, the apostles.

3. Jesus never denied His Jewishness. While some Christians try to deny the connection between Jesus of Nazareth and the Jews of the world, Jesus never denied His Jewishness. He was born Jewish, He was circumcised on the eighth day in keeping with Jewish tradition. He had His Bar Mitzvah on His thirteenth birthday. He kept the law of Moses. He wore the prayer shawl Moses commanded all Jewish men to wear. He died on the cross with an inscription over His head, "King of the Jews."

4. Christians are to support Israel because it brings the blessings of God to them personally. In Psalm 122:6, King David commands all Christians, "Pray for the peace of Jerusalem: May they prosper who love you." The scriptural principal of personal prosperity is tied to blessing Israel and the city of Jerusalem.

5. God judges the Gentiles for their abuse of the Jews.
God promises to punish the nations that come against Is-
rael (Gen. 12:3). . . .God is rising to judge the nations of
the world based on their treatment of the State of Israel.[7]

Israel is a nation in their own land. Their day of salvation is
rapidly approaching. It behooves every believer in Messiah Jesus to
be following the exhortation we read in Psalm 122:6, "Pray for the
peace of Jerusalem." For as we pray for that peace, we are in reality praying for the Prince of Peace to come and rule and reign over
his people Israel and over the entire world as well. "Amen. Come,
Lord Jesus" (Revelation 22:20).

Chapter Notes

1. Ray Bachman, *The God Who Remembers*, Morning Star Ministries,
    Mountain Home, AR, © 2014, pp. 11-24 (entire chapter as edited).
2. John F. Walvoord, *Major Bible Prophecies*, Harper Paperbacks, New
    York, NY, © 1991, p. 190
3. Hal Lindsey, *The Everlasting Hatred, the Roots of Jihad,* Oracle Pub-
    lishing House, Murrieta, CA, © 2002, p. 34
4. Ron Rhodes, *The Popular Dictionary of Bible Prophecy,* Harvest
    House Publishers, Eugene, OR, © 2010, pp. 175f.
5. Elwood McQuaid, *The Zion Connection,* Harvest House, Eugene, OR,
    © 1996, p. 82.
6. Ibid., p. 136f.
7. John Hagee, *Jerusalem Countdown*, Front Line, Lake Mary, FL, ©
    2006, pp. 196-201.

Study Two

The Roots Support the Tree[1]

To fully understand our identity as believers in Jesus, we must do so in light of our spiritual roots in Judaism

All around the home where I grew up on Hawpatch Street in the small north Indiana town of LaGrange were giant maple trees, as was common on almost every street in town. These were very tall trees, many reaching sixty to seventy feet or more into the air, providing an abundance of welcome shade to temper the often extreme summer heat. In the autumn, there was an abundance of leaves which were not so welcome to my father but which we kids enjoyed immensely. These stately trees had lined the streets of our town for decades, probably for more than a hundred years.

Interestingly enough, in all my years of growing up, I don't recall that one of those beautiful trees was ever blown over. Somehow, in spite of their height and breadth, they stood firm in the face of storms year after year. How can that be? Surely, the only ready answer is that they were held firmly by their root system. I have been told that a tree's roots usually extend at least as far underground as the crown of the tree is wide. That means, in essence, we only see half a tree. The other half is underground feeding the part we see and holding it steady against all the pressures that come upon it above ground.

I tell all this obvious and well-known detail to make a vital point in our study of drastic discipleship in the book of Acts. It is nothing less than totally amazing that the exuberant growth of the early church coupled with the raging winds of persecution did not cause it to topple. While we are often excited to see a growth rate of ten percent in our congregations, the early Church saw increases which often ran into the hundreds of percentage points. On the day of Pentecost alone, there were 120 disciples in the morning and by day's end 3,000 more had been added. That's a one day growth rate of 2,500 percent.

How could this new Christian *tree* avoid being so top-heavy that it collapsed of its own weight? The obvious answer is that it was held intact by its roots, even in the face of the intense persecution which was so soon to come against it. What were those roots and are they still important to the Church today? The answer is that they are Jewish roots and they are far more important to us today than most of us believe or realize.

The statement is often made that Pentecost was the birthday of the Church which would seem to indicate that it was a brand new organism. If that were true, it would have no roots; it would be an entirely fresh creation in and of itself. But the Church did have roots and they were deep roots. They were the roots of the Old Testament stretching all the way back to Adam and especially from the time of Abraham forward. Often, when I mention some aspect of Old testament life or law, I am promptly reprimanded and told that what I have said is Old Testament and no longer applies since we are a New Testament Church. That is really a bit of heresy. We are either a Bible church that includes both the Old and New Testaments or we are no church at all.

The Apostle Paul makes this clear when he writes to the church at Rome. He has explained to them that Israel is likened to an olive tree and that Gentile believers have been grafted into that tree as unnatural branches. Then he warns them not to become conceited over their position with these words:

> ...and you, though a wild olive shoot, have been grafted in among the others and now share in the nourishing sap from the olive root, do not boast over those branches. If you do, consider this: You do not support the root, but the root supports you (Romans 11:17bf).

So there we have the answer, clear and direct from another place in the Word of God. How did this play out in the life and teaching of the early Church? Did it make a difference? Did they forthrightly enunciate this truth to their hearers or was it just a matter to be considered by the leadership? When we read the book of Acts, even in a cursory way, we will quickly discover much more teaching about the Hebraic roots of the Christian faith than we had ever imagined.

Before we begin an in-depth look at those portions of Acts which articulate the strength of the Hebrew roots of the Christian faith, we must scrutinize one of the most non-biblical doctrines that has ever been foisted upon the Church of Jesus. This will explain why so many of us have been so unaware of much of end-times prophecy and almost totally ignorant of God's plan for the Jews as we face the conclusion of this present age.

Replacement Theology

As I began to study and learn more about God's prophetic message as we find it throughout the Bible, I was compelled to begin to teach those things I was discovering after many years of ignorance. I was quite amazed to find that my lack of understanding of this entire area of Biblical teaching was widespread and shared by many others. People began to say that they had been in the Church all their lives and had never heard these things. They often commented that their congregations were never taught even the most basic truths of Bible prophecy, and casual mentions of such doctrines were not accompanied by any elaboration or application. How could this be?

The nasty little secret is a huge doctrine which is seldom spoken of in our churches but which underlies much of the way in which we interpret Holy Scripture. That doctrine is commonly called Replacement Theology, although it has more glorious sounding names, such as Supercessionism, which we will not take time to explore at this juncture..

The bottom line is that this doctrine teaches that because of their rejection of Jesus as the Jewish Messiah when He came, the Jews have been condemned by God and have been replaced in God's eternal plan by the Christian Church. Therefore, God has no further plan for the Jews in end-times prophecy. This teaching was promoted as early as the third century by Origen, the Christian teacher and theologian from Alexandria, and later strongly taught by Martin Luther. Under the teaching of Augustine, the Roman Catholic Church adopted this doctrine and as late as Vatican Council II in 1965 it was said, "The Church is the new people of God." In other words, God has broken the promises He made to the Jews in the covenants we find in the Old Testament and which we noted in Study One of this book.

The great problem for us is, if God can break His covenant promises with Israel, then He is also free to break His promises with us in the New Covenant through Jesus Christ. The major difficulty with this is that it runs entirely contrary to the nature of God Himself. If His Word cannot be trusted, then we have nothing to which we can hold. The doctrine makes God a father of lies. We know, therefore, that it cannot be true. What God says in the beginning we can count on to be true to the end.

The practical application for us is that the Old Testament is true in its entirety and therefore pertinent to us as we consider the Jewish roots of the Christian faith. We are not free to pick and choose our roots, anymore than I can randomly select which of my ancestors I would like to include in my family tree. There is much we can determine about our fruitfulness in the future, but nothing at all we can do about our roots.

There is much anti-Semitism in the world today and its growth is quite apparent. The Semites are the descendents of Shem, Noah's son, and were originally called shemites, later changed to Semites. It is especially evident in the Muslim nations where we hear declarations of those who desire to wipe Israel off the map. Unfortunately, there is also much evidence of Jewish hatred within the Christian Church. This is not surprising when we consider the generations of people in our churches who have been indoctrinated with the un-Biblical doctrine of Replacement Theology.

It behooves us then to give careful attention to the roots of our faith as they were spelled out to the first generation of believers. We will look at our roots under a number of categories instead of focusing on them in the chronological way they are presented in the Acts.

The Roots in History

We readily see ample material in Acts to enable us to grasp how important the early Church leaders felt it was to connect believers with the ancient Hebraic roots of the faith. We will especially examine the lengthy recitation of Jewish history by Stephen as he stood before the Sanhedrin, the Jewish ruling council, as recorded in chapter seven. We will also see in chapter thirteen the more abbreviated narrative of the Apostle Paul when he was in Antioch.

Stephen exhibited a powerful ability to persuade people to follow Jesus, not only by words but by signs and wonders that were clearly visible to the people. But this success aroused much animosity and by securing the untrue testimony of men who claimed to have heard Stephen blaspheming God, he was ultimately brought before the Sanhedrin in a kind of trial. The high priest asked him if the charges were true. Stephen grasped the opportunity to speak and declared to the leaders whom he called "Brothers and fathers" (7:2) **[Note: when no book reference is given in this chapter, the reference is in Acts]** this extended version of Jewish history.

He wasted no time in making the connection between what he was doing and what God had done in the past. He immediately began by telling of God's call to Abraham and continued with Abraham's story after being instructed by God, going to Canaan, having descendents Isaac and Jacob, and then the 400 year sojourn in Egypt including the complete story of Moses and ultimately the Exodus.

Stephen told of the prophecy of exile in Babylon and went on to remember the wilderness tabernacle and David's vision for the Temple in Jerusalem followed by its ultimate construction by Solomon. As he concludes his synopsis of Jewish history, he refers to his hearers as "You stiff-necked people, with uncircumcised hearts and ears! You are just like your fathers: You always resist the Holy Spirit" (7:51).

Stephen's wrath comes to full head as he finally arrives at telling in a sentence about Jesus. He asks a question of the Sanhedrin and then gives a final damning declaration:

> "Was there ever a prophet your fathers did not persecute? They even killed those who predicted the coming of the Righteous One. And now you have betrayed and murdered him [Jesus the Righteous One]" (7:52).

This testimony resulted in the stoning death of Stephen to be quickly forthcoming, but we dare not miss a most important factor in this episode. Without doubt, Stephen realized this was his last opportunity to make a most profound statement about what this new movement, centered around the crucified and risen Jesus, was all about. He placed it firmly in connection with all of Jewish history.

This was not a new thing or a start-up religion; it was the ongoing work of God in dealing with man.

We might well say that the reason Stephen went into all this historical detail was that he was speaking to the Sanhedrin, a wholly Jewish group of religious leaders. It was important for them to know the relationship, but that is not the totality of the event. Others would hear this in addition to the Jewish leadership. Stephen understood that the work of reaching mankind which God began with His call to Abraham, He was now continuing in the person of His own Son, Jesus. The cap sheaf of Stephen's testimony were the words. "Look, I see heaven open and the Son of Man standing at the right hand of God" (7:56).

When we begin our understanding of the Christian faith with the New Testament and in effect jettison all that God has done as recorded in the former account, we impoverish ourselves immensely. Stephen's testimony clearly set forth the intimate kinship between what we refer to as the Jewish faith and the Christian faith. The events and teaching we find in the book of Acts serve as a bridge to help us make this connection. It was clear in the minds of the early Apostles that the rapid growth of the Church was only possible when understood in light of the Jewish roots which provided support.

We find another wonderful stating of the background of the Church's foundation in Judaism in the teaching of Paul when he was in Pisidian Antioch in northern Syria. They went to the synagogue on the Sabbath, Saturday not Sunday, and Paul was asked by the synagogue leaders to give a message to encourage the people. As Paul begins to speak, he makes a statement which is most apropos to our present discussion. He addressed his hearers as "Men of Israel and you Gentiles who worship God" (13:16).

How often we run over a phrase and fail to comprehend that it is saying something highly significant. Such is the case with Paul carefully addressing both Jews and Gentiles before he explains that the new dynamic believers in Jesus are equally related to Jewish history as are the Jews themselves. What a revelation! This is so important that Paul addresses the same issue in his epistles, especially the letter to the Christians at Rome which we will study in detail in Study Five.

As Paul spells out in abbreviated form the history of the Hebrews, he covers all the highlights of their history beginning with God's choosing of the Hebrews as a people and moving on quickly to include the time in Egypt, the desert wanderings and ultimately the conquering of Canaan. He tells briefly of the judges, the prophets and the kings ending with David. He then leaps to make the essential connection of Jesus to David by saying,

> *"From this man's descendants God has brought to Israel the Savior Jesus as he promised"* (13:23).

So Paul links Jesus to being the expected Messiah of the Jews. But was He for the Jews only? Just in case Paul's hearers had missed earlier to whom he was making his encouraging comments, He repeats in slightly different phraseology:

> *"Brothers, children of Abraham, and you God-fearing Gentiles, it is to us that this message of salvation has been sent. . . .We tell you good news: What God promised our fathers he has fulfilled for us, their children, by raising up Jesus"* (13:26, 32, 33a).

So there we have it, distinctly and forthrightly; through Jesus all believers whether Jew or Gentile are intimately linked together by their common roots based firmly in history. What seems so innately clear to those early believers, has been lost along the way. Christians must again claim the life and strength which are rightly ours through our common roots.

The Roots Fulfilled in Jesus

Closely akin to seeing the novice Church in the historical context of its Jewish roots is that of recognizing Jesus as the fulfillment of God's promises of a coming Messiah. We find this theme arising quickly as we read the Acts account. On the day of Pentecost, Peter addresses this issue head-on:

> *"'Men of Israel, listen to this: Jesus of Nazareth was a man accredited by God to you by miracles, wonders and signs which God did among you through him, . . .Therefore let all Israel be assured of this: God has made this Jesus, whom you crucified, both Lord and Christ'"* (2:22, 36).

The word translated as *Christ* was literally meaning the "anointed one" and would readily be understood by the Jewish hearers as referring to Messiah. In this case, Peter was addressing only the Jews, as they were the ones being unable to recognize Jesus as their long-awaited Messiah. In our day the reverse is true; it is the Gentiles who need to understand that Jesus is the fulfillment of the Jewish Messiah. It is not inappropriate for Christians to refer to Jesus not only as the Christ, but as *Yeshua ha Mashiach*, Jesus the Messiah.

A crippled beggar was healed and this brought quite a crowd of onlookers to discover what was happening. Peter grasped the opportunity to again explain who Jesus was with powerful words of explanation and exhortation:

> *"The God of Abraham, Isaac and Jacob, the God of our fathers, has glorified his servant Jesus. You disowned the Holy and Righteous One . . . You killed the author of life, but God raised him from the dead. . . .But this is how God fulfilled what he had foretold through all the prophets, saying that his Christ would suffer. Repent then and turn to God, so that your sins may be wiped out"* (3:13-15, 18f).

Jesus Himself had proclaimed, after his resurrection, this same truth, so the issue of the Old Testament being fulfilled in Christ was not a surprise to them. Jesus had said,

> *"This is what I told you while I was still with you: Everything must be fulfilled that is written about me in the Law of Moses, the Prophets and the Psalms"* (Luke 24:44).

Thus, when the apostles taught that all things were fulfilled in Jesus and that He was the promised and expected Messiah they were not just expressing an opinion of their own; they were telling what they had learned from Jesus Himself. It is essential that we understand the difference between fulfillment and replacement. Neither Jesus nor any of the early teachers of the Church taught that Jesus was replacing the Old Testament Scriptures. They were not being done away with, they found their fullness in Jesus. Therefore, every believer in Jesus, no matter what he has been taught by his church or denomination, must come to the realization that Replacement Theology is untrue. The roots of our salvation are firmly planted in the Law, the Prophets and the Psalms, just as Jesus declared.

Let us briefly explore a couple of additional instances of how we see the fulfillment of the Hebraic roots in Jesus. Peter and John had been instruments which God had used in the healing of the crippled beggar. As they put forth their defense, they again appealed to their Jewish roots saying,

> *"It is by the name of Jesus Christ of Nazareth, whom you crucified but whom God raised from the dead, that this man stands before you healed. He [Jesus] is 'the stone you builders rejected, which has become the capstone'"* (4:10bf).

The quote about the stone is directly from Psalm 118:22. What makes it especially interesting is that once again the apostles are not only quoting the fulfillment of an Old Testament prophecy, they are also following the example of Jesus who used this same quotation in referring to Himself in Matthew 21:42. Jesus had no presumption whatsoever that He was replacing anything of the Old Testament but only bringing it to its fullness.

Another exciting reference to Jesus and prophetic fulfillment is found in Acts chapter eight. The Ethiopian in his chariot had been reading Isaiah 53:7f, concerning the sacrificial lamb, when God brought Phillip his way. The Ethiopian asked to whom the prophet was referring and Phillip jumped at the opportunity to answer "and told him the good news about Jesus" (8:35). Phillip understood the Hebraic roots of Christianity.

What does this say to us? Surely it means that if we would fully understand the message and person of Jesus, we must be careful to do so in the context of our Jewish roots. As we attempt to study Bible prophecy, we also find that unless we understand our roots, we will never come to correct conclusions about the meaning of the prophetic message for the future, because all the prophecies find their fulfillment and meaning in the person of Jesus Himself.

The Roots in Action

Had the Apostles and other early Church leaders intended to create a chasm of distinction between the new body of believers and the former roots in Judaism, they could have easily done so. But they did not! Despite the great and wonderful new thing that God was accomplishing in the followers of Jesus, there was no attempt to distance themselves from their roots, even in the face of intense opposition from the Jewish leadership. They instead continued in their actions on a day-to-day basis with their new evangelistic activities closely entwined with their observance of many of their former Jewish routines. Interestingly enough, this did not cause a spiritual schizophrenic problem for themselves. Rather, they evidenced in a powerful way that they at last had it all together.

Perhaps the thing that brought a sense of unity and purpose to the early church could be of great benefit to us as well. Let's notice a list of the ways in which their Hebraic roots became evident as they engaged in drastic discipleship of making new disciples and equipping them to make more disciples.

They recognized the importance of the Sabbath as noted with at least nine references to the day enjoined to be observed by the fourth Commandment. They reckoned their week by the Sabbath

(23:44 & 17:2); they engaged in certain activities on the Sabbath (13:14 & 15:21). They referred to distance by the Biblical standard of a "Sabbath day's journey" (1:12). Their roots were not lost in their exciting new venture.

The seven feasts of God, which were given to the Jews to observe special events, also continued in significance. These holy observances were markers in the year which were not dismissed as no longer appropriate. That the Feasts remained of importance can be seen by an event recorded in Acts 12. When King Herod saw that his persecution of Christian leaders pleased many of the Jews, he arrested Peter. We read that "this happened during the Feast of Unleavened Bread" and "intended to bring him out for public trial after the Passover" (12:3f). Study Four is a more detailed account of how we see Jesus fulfilling the seven feasts which God ordained.

Pentecost, without doubt, has become the primary Feast with which Christians are familiar. Indeed, for many, it is probably the only one known. The Church took it over as a Christian holy day because of the momentous event that took place on that Jewish Feast day. That was the day on which Jesus poured out His Holy Spirit on the Church to anoint it with power for the overwhelming task of making drastic disciples in a very hostile world.

The Feast of Pentecost had originally been given by God as a day in which to bring an offering to Him to celebrate the wheat harvest. For Christians it became a day to commemorate the beginning of a mighty harvest of souls into the Kingdom of God through the Gospel of Christ Jesus. The proper understanding of our entire ministry hinges on our knowledge of our relationship to our Jewish roots.

We find another case in which we see evidence of the importance of the Feast days in Acts 20. There it tells the story of Paul making his farewell to the Ephesian church and concluding with these words: "he was in a hurry to reach Jerusalem, if possible, by the Day of Pentecost" (20:16). The record is quite plain. The early Church remained attached to its roots and that certainly can be interpreted to suggest that the church of today might also find strength for its task if it were to be more closely in touch with its foundation in Judaism.

Am I saying here that we must begin to celebrate the Feasts appointed by God for Israel and to slavishly observe the weekly Sabbath? Not at all, though more and more believers in Jesus do find that to be a helpful exercise. What I am saying is that at minimum we need to be cognizant of more of the Judaical background from which the New Covenant came. By studying more of the Old Testament, we will discover that doors of understanding of the New Testament narrative will be more widely opened

For instance, the knowing that the Spring Feasts of Passover, Unleavened Bread and First Fruits were fulfilled by Jesus in His death, burial and resurrection will broaden our understanding of these sacred Jewish traditions. It will also shed new light on our concepts of who Jesus is both as the Jewish Messiah and the Christian Savior. Recognizing that Jesus fulfilled the Feast of Pentecost by pouring out His Spirit on the Church helps us to know our role between His first Advent and His return in power and great glory.

Also, recognizing how precisely Jesus fulfilled the first four Feasts will give us increased hope of the exactness of how He will also bring fullness to the three Fall Feasts of Trumpets, Day of Atonement and Tabernacles. These we can confidently expect to see fulfilled in His Second Coming, the salvation of all Israel and His dwelling among His people during His one thousand year Millennial reign here on earth. Yes, our Jewish roots have much help and support to render to us if we will avail ourselves of the opportunity to become aware of their value.

The Roots and Our Future

The final aspect of our Jewish roots we shall peruse shall be a bit about their relationship to the days ahead, especially those rapidly approaching days that we often refer to as the End-Times, or the events especially surrounding the second advent of the Messiah. Since the church was just in its infancy and was experiencing burgeoning growth, their attention was understandably focused on proclaiming Jesus as Savior and explaining who He really was. They also had their hands full of very practical problems for which they had no experience or background upon which to draw. But we do find several instances of teaching that relate to the latter days.

The prophetic future was definitely on the Apostles' minds as the Acts record begins. They had a most probing question for Jesus which was not too unlike their conversation with the Master one day on the Mount of Olives (Luke 21, Matthew 24). This time they phrased their query most succinctly, "'Lord, are you at this time going to restore the kingdom to Israel?'" (1:6). This was a question directly relating to what they knew of Biblical prophecy. Jesus deferred His answer by telling them that they had work to do in the immediate future, and thus at that time they need not know specific dates and times. The point, however, is that these prophetic concerns were in the forefront of their minds.

54

While not a direct answer, they were in only a short time given a confirmation of a marvelous prophetic truth. Immediately after their short conversation, Jesus was taken up to heaven. With eyes barely daring to believe what they had just seen, they focused on the spot where they had seen their Lord disappear. It was then that two white-robed men spoke to them:

> *"Men of Galilee," they said, "why do you stand here looking into the sky? This same Jesus who was taken from you into heaven, will come back in the same way you have seen him go into heaven"* (1:11).

We often pass over this verse acknowledging it as important but seldom realizing that this is one of the most fully packed verses of Bible prophecy in the New Testament. Think of the truths stated here. The long awaited Messiah when He comes will be this same Jesus who just left. That He is in heaven tells us where His present ministry is taking place. Paul confirms this by saying, "Christ Jesus who died . . . is at the right hand of God and is also interceding for us" (Romans 8:34). Stephen confirmed this, as immediately prior to his death, "'Look,' he said, 'I see heaven open and the Son of Man standing at the right hand of God'" (7:56).

Many people are very doubtful that Jesus will ever return, but the clear word here is that "he will come back." And he will come back "in the same way you have seen him go." How was that? He went in His glorified body; He will return in His glorified body. He left as a person; He will return as a person. He left from the Mount of Olives; He will return to the Mount of Olives. He left his new Bride, the Church; one day He will return for His Bride.

So it is clear that as the new Church set forth on its ministry, it was already beginning to long for the return of Jesus.

As the manifestations of the Holy Spirit's presence began to be noticed, great questioning began to take place with many asking in perplexity just what this all meant. This gave Peter the opportunity to begin to share the message of Jesus. But he did not begin with Jesus; he instead spoke first about why they were seeing and hearing the disciples speaking about God's working in this brand new way. To explain it, Peter immediately went to the Old Testament prophet Joel. He quoted these now familiar words.

"In the last days, God says, I will pour out my Spirit on all people. Your sons and daughters will prophecy, your young men will see visions, your old men will dream dreams. Even on my servants, both men and women, I will pour out my Spirit in those days, and they will prophesy'" (2:17f from Joel 2:28-32).

This quite readily explained that what people were experiencing was a new movement of God's Holy Spirit. However, Peter did not stop after verse 18 but went on to quote more of the message of Joel concerning unusual physical manifestations that would occur both in the heavens and on the earth in the last days. This poses a problem for us. While the Spirit's work was immediately observable from the Day of Pentecost onward, there were no unique signs in either the heavens or on earth on that day. Was Peter incorrect in quoting what he did or is there something else for us here to learn? Actually we have here a wonderful illustration of how to use and interpret Bible prophecy. If we are to be able understand and properly teach prophetic Scriptures, we must acquire some basic knowledge of how to do so. This is an unique and excellent demonstration of that.

One necessary principle to grasp is that prophecy may be fulfilled in a number of different ways. First of all, it may all be fulfilled at the same time. For instance, the prophecy that Jesus would be born in the town of Bethlehem Ephrata was totally fulfilled at His first coming. We need not look for any more Messiahs to be born in Bethlehem. However, some prophecies may find more than one fulfillment. In this particular case, I believe that we may expect another great outpouring of the Spirit when all Israel recognizes Jesus as the Messiah at His Second Coming when Paul says, "All Israel will be saved" (Romans 11:26).

A third way of interpretation is that a portion of a prophecy may be fulfilled and the remainder not find fulfillment until a later time. Such is the case with Peter's quote from Joel. The portion about the Spirit's work was fulfilled on the Day of Pentecost, but the descriptions about the wonders and signs in the heavens and on earth are reserved until just prior to the Second Coming of Messiah at the end of the Tribulation period.

The importance of this in light of our discussion in this chapter is that at the outset, the Apostles were planting in the minds and spirits of those early disciples that their Jewish roots extended not only to time past but also into the future. To fully understand our identity, we must do so in light of our spiritual roots in Judaism. Those roots are still our supportive base and they will continue to be so forever. To fail to study and teach the Old Testament prophecies is to severely impoverish both our spiritual heritage and our future expectations. Elwood McQuaid makes a strong case for viewing Scripture through Jewish eyes.

Evangelicals have no question that Jesus of Nazareth was a Jew. When properly seen, this impacts dramatically His view of the Scriptures and how they should be interpreted. . . .Recognizing that Christ was brought to us as a Jew buttresses the concept that, if this is true, the Scriptures can be best understood by studying them through the historical and cultural context in which they were given.[2]

Peter made a strong case for identifying the oneness that exists when he appeared before the Council at Jerusalem to argue the case for accepting Gentiles into the Church. We tend to forget that in the beginning it was a Jewish Church which believed in Jesus and there was uncertainty whether Gentiles could be a part of it. How reversed is our thinking today. Peter made some telling statements as he made his case.

"God who knows the heart, showed that he accepted them [Gentiles] just as he did us [Jews]. He made no distinction between us and them, for he purified their hearts by faith. . . .We believe that it is through the grace of our Lord Jesus that we are saved, just as they are" (15:8, 9, 11).

In that same presentation, Peter again calls upon one of the prophets, this time Amos, to suggest some of what would take place in the very last days. Listen to what is said will come to pass:

"'After this I will return and rebuild David's fallen tent. Its ruins I will rebuild and I will restore it, that the remnant of men may seek the Lord, and all the Gentiles who bear my name, says the Lord, who does these things that have been known for ages'" (15:16-18 from Amos 9:11-12).

So those engaged in drastic discipleship from the very beginning were looking forward to the return of Messiah based on their understanding of the ancient prophets. As followers of Jesus today, it behooves us to be as diligent to proclaim not only the message of salvation, but also the message of expectation about future events. If God has great plans for the Jewish people as we come increasingly closer to the end-times, what implication does this hold for Christians? What are we to be doing in this same regard. Michael Evans has a strong word for us in answer to these queries.

We have a date with destiny! When we support Israel we are supporting the only nation that was created by an act of God. We are declaring the Bible is true, that God is not a promise-breaker and that the royal land grant given to Abraham and his seed through Isaac and Jacob was an everlasting and unconditional covenant.

"Comfort , yes, comfort My people!" Says your God. "Speak comfort to Jerusalem, and cry out to her; That her warfare is ended, That her iniquity is pardoned; For she has received from the Lord's hand double for all her sins" (Isaiah 40:1-2).

This prophetic word is a God-given mandate to Christians to offer comfort, encouragement, and emotional and financial support to the suffering House of Israel. If this scripture is not for Christians, then for whom? Nation after nation has turned its back on the Jewish people—we cannot do the same.[3]

Much of the Church has found Bible prophecy difficult and so either ignored it or spiritualized it to make it a more simple and easier to comprehend its message, but in either case it constitutes a failure to teach the entirety of what God wants His people to know. Oh, that we might be able to join our voice with that of the Apostle Paul and proclaim, "'I declare to you today that I am innocent of the blood of all men. For I have not hesitated to proclaim to you the whole will of God'" (20:26f).

We could continue to cite other examples of how the early disciples understood the impact of the Jewish roots upon the new Church. Then as now, the Body of Christ is dependent upon its roots. When we fail to grasp the important significance of this truth, we leave ourselves in a spiritually weakened position. When we realize who we are, we can claim with authority that which the Apostle Paul used to encourage the believers at Ephesus:

> *"This mystery* [a truth formerly unknown but now revealed] *is that through the gospel the Gentiles are heirs together with Israel, members together in one body, and sharers together in the promise in Christ Jesus"* (Ephesians 3:6 explanatory phrase added).

It is nothing less than amazing how succinctly the Apostle summarizes and emphasizes the value of knowing our Hebraic roots and allowing ourselves to be supported and nourished by them.

For Reflection or Group Discussion

1. Why do you think so many Christians are quite unaware of the relationship of the Christian faith to its Jewish roots?
2. When you consider what your congregation teaches about Jewish history and end-times prophecy, do you feel your church en-

dorses the doctrine of Replacement Theology? What specific reasons can you cite for your answer?

3. How has the way you have heard Bible stories taught and preached affected your understanding of the relationship of the Church to its Hebrew roots?

4. Thinking of Steven's and Paul's presentations of the Jewish roots of the faith, how could we better go about our teaching in the Church?

5. If you were asked by someone to explain the relationship of Christianity and Judaism, how would you go about it?

6. What particular things of the Jewish faith would you especially like to learn more about?

7. Since almost all Old Testament prophecy was written to the Jews, how can we better learn to understand God's plan for what are commonly called the End Times?

8. In what way did the author's presentation of Bible prophecy interpretation aid your understanding? What aspects of prophecy would you like to know more fully?

9. In what practical way can you use the information contained in this chapter to encourage your friends and acquaintances?

Chapter Notes

1. Ray Bachman, *Drastic Discipleship*, Morning Star Ministries, Mountain Home, AR, © 2013, pp. 143-166 (entire chapter with editing).

2. Elwood McQuaid, *The Zion Connection*, Harvest House, Eugene, OR, © 1996, p. 143.

3. Michael D. Evans, *Beyond Iraq*, White Stone Books, Lakeland, FL, © 2003, pp. 120, 121.

Study Three

Did Jesus Have A Wife?[1]

Did Jesus have a wife when He walked this earth? Did He find a woman to love who became His life partner? If so, who was she? What happened to her after His crucifixion and resurrection? Do we have any love letters Jesus sent? Why do we find no mention of His marriage in the Bible?

For many Christians, these are questions which they have never been asked. These are issues that they have never heard discussed and which in honesty they prefer not to hear discussed. Most believers and non-believers alike would likely answer the first question with a resounding, "No, of course, Jesus never had a wife."

And that, of course, is a correct answer if when we ask the question we are referring to Jesus taking a woman in physical marriage during the years He was on the earth at the time of His first coming. But, is there more to the question than that? Do we need to be looking at the subject from a broader perspective? The answer may be far more exciting than we have anticipated.

The writings of Dan Brown sparked much debate a few years, ago ,especially his book, *The Da Vinci Code*. In this book, which is a novel but supposedly based on research and fact, Brown sets forth the proposition that Jesus was indeed married and that His wife was none other than Mary Magdalene. And not only were they married, according to Brown, but they had children. Thus, there was a royal bloodline that has been carried on even until today by the offspring of Jesus and Mary Magdalene. Indeed, that is the theme of *The Da Vinci Code* as the author states: "Mary Magdalene carried the bloodline of Jesus Christ."[2]

Of course, Dan Brown did not find his substantiation for his book from *The Bible*. He used as his sources many other books that had been written as "gospels" but which were not judged as divinely inspired and authentic by those who determined under the leadership of the Holy Spirit which writings would comprise the Holy Scriptures.

Brown's attitude is that writings which gave insight into the earthly side of Jesus were not included because they would tear down many of the teachings of the Catholic Church. He says of these non-canonical gospels, "'...any gospels that described earthly aspects of Jesus' life had to be omitted from the Bible. Unfortunately for the early editors, one particularly troubling earthly theme kept recurring in the gospels, Mary Magdalene.' He paused. 'More specifically, her marriage to Jesus Christ.'"[3]

Brown goes on to say, "'Moreover, Jesus as a married man makes infinitely more sense than our standard biblical view of Jesus as a bachelor.'"[4] He is joined in this line of thought by another writer who is fixated on Mary Magdalene as the wife of Jesus. Margaret Starbird writes, "In the first century in the culture to which Jesus belonged, a man's marriage was virtually taken for granted."[5] So, here we come to the crux of the issue. To say Jesus was married because it makes sense culturally misses the real dynamic of who Jesus was. If there is anything He wasn't, it was being tied to the culture and being politically correct. To argue from culture is to not understand who Jesus is and what He was about when He came into our world. He transformed old practices and traditions and infused them with new and vibrant meaning.

There is no doubt that Mary Magdalene was a key figure among the disciples of Jesus. She very likely was His closest female follower, aside from His mother, as is evidenced by the Scriptural record. However, that is a far cry from jumping to the conclusion that their closeness can be interpreted to mean that they were husband and wife. But Brown continues to assert that that was the case as is shown in this bit of dialogue from his novel. "'Not only was Jesus Christ married, but He was a father, my dear. Mary Magdalene was the Holy Vessel....She was the womb that bore the lineage, and the vine from which the sacred fruit sprang forth.'"[6]

Such writings as these run in diametrical opposition to the Biblical record upon which Christians have firmly stood since the New Testament writings were recognized by the Church by early in the second century as the authentic, Holy Spirit inspired Word of God. Starbird, whose book *The Woman With the Alabaster Jar—Mary Magdalene and the Holy Grail* was a primary source book for Dan Brown, wrote in her later book, "...the other answer, confirmed by left-handed intuitives who see visions and dream dreams, asserts that Mary Magdalene was the bride so long exiled from our consciousness."[7]

Thus, the thrust of Brown, Starbird and others is that the fact of the marriage of Jesus has been hidden for all these two thousand years. That only a few were aware of this royal marriage. And that Mary of Magdala has been waiting in exile for the world to recognize her highly exalted state as the wife of the Son of God. She is in anticipation of us giving her a great wedding reception.

But Mary could not be the Bride of Christ for He has another Bride chosen for Him by His Father God before the foundation of the world. Who is this authentic Bride of God's only Son?

When Dan Brown's book appeared, followed shortly afterward by a Hollywood movie version, there were a multitude of responses to his theories by many scholars who recognized the inherent impact upon those who had held to the truth that Jesus had not taken a wife for Himself while in the world.

One of those responses sums up well our understanding of this controversy.

> *"This preposterous lie of this mythical marriage of Jesus and Mary Magdalene is not to advance a better understanding of marriage, or advance a deep appreciation for the feminine.*
> *"I'll tell you what it is for. It is solely to destroy the truth about the covenantal union between God and man that has taken place in the marriage between Jesus and His true bride, the Church. 'The Da Vinci Code' is quite simply an <u>end time heresy </u>attacking the <u>rapture</u> of the Church and attacking the doctrine of the <u>Bride of Christ.</u>*
> *"...Yes, Jesus will be married—not to a woman, but to all of us who constitute the bride of Christ."[8]*

The time is quickly approaching when this momentous event will take place. Now is an appropriate occasion for all believers in the Lord Jesus to begin to sing with longing hearts the words of expectation made popular by the Cathedral Quartet:

> *Is that wedding music I hear?*
> *The bride's adorned and waiting to appear.*
> *There's heavenly preparation*
> *For a wedding celebration.*
> *Is that wedding music that I hear?*
>
> *The family is prepared for a wedding,*
> *All have been invited to attend*
> *The Bride stands ready, waiting for a signal;*
> *When the Groom says, "Rise my children,   come on in."*
>
> *Soon we'll rise to leave this land of sorrow*
> *For that silver morning in the air.*
> *The Father's hand will lead us*
> *To the holy land of splendor.*
> *Have you made your preparation to go there?*[9]

Yes, the Lord Jesus has selected a Bride. The wedding date is approaching and the Bride is making herself ready. To assist her in her wedding preparations, Jesus has written a series of love letters to his betrothed. We find these in the second and third chapters of Revelation

But first we need to lay some foundation for our understanding of the relationship that exists between this heavenly Bridegroom and His earth-bound Bride. The Bible clearly teaches that God Himself sees His relationship with His followers as that of husband and wife.

God and His Betrothed

We may find it difficult to quickly grasp the idea of Jesus having a Bride because we have grown accustomed to thinking of Him as unmarried from all our knowledge of the stories in the Bible of His life. While in many cultures and religions, the marriage of the gods plays an important role in their understanding of what their deity is like, that concept is not a part of our thinking as Christians..

So we find the idea of a marrying God quite a stretch for our minds. It would be not difficult to accept the concept of Jesus having an earthly wife if we didn't believe Him to be the very Son of God. But that, indeed, is who He is.

We walk a tightrope in our understanding of Jesus. On the one hand, we are tempted to see Him as One like ourselves. We make Him in our image. We understand Him in terms of who we are. We expect Him to be like all other men. That is the tragic mistake of Dan Brown and his ilk: because all good Jewish boys in the first century took wives, therefore Jesus must have taken a wife. When we travel down the wrong road, we arrive at the wrong destination.

Jesus was fully human. The Apostle Paul said, "God sent his Son, born of a woman, born under the law, to redeem those under law, that we might receive the full rights of sons" (Galatians 4:4). But, having said that Jesus was truly a human male, we have not at all defined Him. He was also fully God. Therefore, He spoke, acted, and taught as the divine creator, not only of man but of the entire universe. He lived out His life in the flesh that we might understand who He was in the Spirit.

When we see Jesus strictly in human terms, we miss who He truly is. He is the heavenly lover who claims a Bride for Himself out of the people of the earth. He is not primarily an example for us. He is the One who desires a relationship with us that is so intimate that He describes it as the husband/wife union. Let's look at the Biblical background for such an understanding.

The book of the prophet Hosea gives us perhaps the clearest statements from God about how He views the relationship of Himself with His people. He tells Hosea to take for himself a wife who is an adulterous woman (Hosea 1:2). He had the Prophet take this drastic step to provide a living representation of the people of God, "...because the land is guilty of vilest adultery in departing from the Lord" (Hosea 1:2).

When Moses was given the Ten Commandments, the seventh stated simply and without any qualifications, "You shall not commit adultery" (Exodus 20:14). People then and now understand that to mean you are not to leave your marriage partner for another. So, when God judges the nation of Israel to be adulterous, He is saying that they have left the One to whom they are married. But God tells the nation through Hosea that He is willing to have them come back to Himself and that when they do, "'In that day,' declares the Lord, 'you will call me 'my husband'" (Hosea 2:16).

It doesn't get much clearer than that. However, God goes on to describe the nature of their marriage:

> *I will betroth you to me forever;*
> *I will betroth you in righteousness and justice, in love and compassion*
> *I will betroth you in faithfulness...* (Hosea 2:19-20).

A betrothal is a promise to marry. God is saying that if people will come to him in trust, He gives them His pledge of fidelity that they will be married to Him. So, it is not surprising that the Lord Jesus would also see Himself as married to His followers.

We find the same message echoed in other Scriptures. In Jeremiah, the message is "Return, faithless people," declares the Lord, "for I am your husband" (Jeremiah 3:14). Through Isaiah, another prophet, God declares, "For your maker is your husband—the Lord Almighty is his name" (Isaiah 54:5).

The fact that Jesus saw Himself married to His followers was not lost on the early Church. In perhaps the most well-known New Testament teaching on Christian marriage, we find words that help us to understand that our human marriages are simply reflections of a greater marriage, that of Jesus and His Church:

> *Wives, submit to your husbands as to the Lord.. For, the husband is the head of the wife as Christ is the head of the church....*
>
> *Husbands, love your wives, just as Christ loved the church and gave himself up for her to make her holy, cleansing her by the washing with water through the word, and to present her to himself as a radiant church...In the same way, husbands ought to love their wives as their own bodies. He who loves his wife loves himself...."For this reason a man will leave his father and mother and be united to his wife, and the two will become one flesh." This is a profound mystery—but I am talking about Christ and the church* (Ephesians 5:23-32).

So here we have a very forthright statement that Jesus is the Bridegroom to which all other bridegrooms must look. The Church is the Bride which all other brides must emulate. Paul is not writing here with the idea that we can learn what the relationship of Jesus to the Church is by saying it is like human marriage. Rather, it is the reverse. We get a full understanding of human marriage by looking at the heavenly Bridegroom and his wife.

This is why at the very outset of Jesus' public ministry we find John the Baptist describing Jesus with the same term. Some of John's disciples came to him with a concern about the fact that Jesus was gaining in popularity and that perhaps John should be offended by this. They said:

> *"Rabbi, that man who was with you on the other side of the Jordan—the one you testified about—well, he is baptizing, and everyone is going to him." To this John replied, "...You yourselves can testify that I said, 'I am not the Christ but am sent ahead of him.' The bride belongs to the bridegroom. The friend who attends the bridegroom waits and listens for him, and is full of joy when he hears the bridegroom's voice. That joy is mine, and it is now complete"* (John 3:26-29).

John had it correct. He recognized Jesus as the Bridegroom. He rightly saw those who were becoming followers of Jesus as those who were being selected to be His Bride. There was no jealousy in John; indeed, he claimed complete joy in what was happening. When we understand the Bride/Groom relationship in its fullness, we too are filled with joy. It enables us to more completely understand the prophetic Scriptures and to be waiting and watching in happy anticipation of Christ's soon return to claim His chosen Bride. If we lose sight of that perspective, it is easy to become discouraged with the decaying nature of life around us. A Swedish hymn writer captured the need to be constantly reflecting upon who we are as a part of the selected Bride.

If you seem empty of any feeling,
Rejoice—you are His ransomed bride!
If those you cherish seem not to love you,
And dark assails from every side,
Still yours the promise, come what may,
In loss and triumph; in laughter, crying,
In want and riches, in living, dying,
That you are purchased as you are.[10]

Even with this understanding, we may yet find a difficulty in comprehending how this all plays out in end-times prophecy. We may find ourselves with a knowledge of the Glorious Appearing of Christ as the Lion of Judah in what we call the Second Coming and still have missed the wonderful truths concerning His return as the awaited Bridegroom. Let's take a look at our Jewish roots and see if we don't find there some marvelous help in knowing what to expect regarding the plans of the Bridegroom. For after all, He is completely Jewish.

The Jewish Wedding Ceremony

For more than twenty years I have used a small booklet called *The Wedding Covenant*[11] with couples planning their wedding ceremony. It contains a most useful list of why we do the traditional things we do in a marriage ceremony along with the meaning and also some attempts to know where the tradition came from. But it also contains an excellent chart of aspects of the Jewish wedding and the relationship of each part to God's salvation plan. I will use that material in assisting us in understanding a most important passage of Scripture which we have often wrongly understood.

We can hear a portion of Scripture read and expounded upon so frequently and in the same context, that we may miss the cutting edge of what it really has to say to us. Such a Scripture is the first four verses of chapter 14 of John's gospel. When was the last time you heard it read and a message preached on it. My strong hunch is that it was at a funeral. Jesus is speaking and says,

> *"Do not let your hearts be troubled. Trust in God; trust also in me. In my Father's house are many rooms; if it were not so, I would have told you. I am going there to prepare a place for you. And if I go and prepare a place for you, I will come back and take you to be with me that you also may be where I am. You know the way to the place where I am going"* (John 14:1-4).

This Scripture has brought comfort to untold thousands of persons and families who have suffered the loss of a loved one. Indeed, it has been used so successfully that many people think that all a person has to do is to die and that then they have this wonderful promise of the presence of Jesus. I believe that many people on the basis of this Scripture believe in a universal salvation in which all people go to heaven when they pass from this earthly life. Nothing could be further from the truth and nothing misses more what Jesus was teaching His disciples.

In the first place, in the Scripture it is Jesus who is going away. We have used this passage to speak of our departed loved ones who have left. Of course, it is true that when Jesus returns, it will be for those who have died having faith in Him as well as for living believers. But it is important that we diligently work to understand Scripture in its context.

Jesus had told the apostles just before the conversation we find in John 14, that He would be leaving them. This had caused them to have troubled spirits. He had said,

> *"My children, I will be with you only a little longer, You will look for me, and just as I told the Jews, so I tell you now: Where I am going, you cannot come"* (John 13:33).

So, to assuage their fears and apprehensions, He gave them words of explanation of where He was going, what He would be doing there, and that He would come back for them. The impact of these words have been lost to us to a great extent because they were spoken in a setting and a culture in which they had a very unique and specific meaning, but with which we are unfamiliar. These words are words directly from the Jewish wedding context: I am going to prepare a place for us to live together as husband and wife and when I have the place completed, I will return and take you to be with me in our new home.

But it was not just from the lips of John the Baptist that the disciples heard Jesus referred to as the Bridegroom. Nor was the night before Jesus went to the cross the initial encounter with the idea of Jesus as the Bridegroom for the apostles. In the same chapter of Mark in which we read of the calling of the twelve, we find recorded that Jesus spoke of Himself using the same designation.

> *Now John's disciples and the Pharisees were fasting. Some people came and asked Jesus, "How is it that John's disciples and the disciples of the Pharisees are fasting, but yours are not?"*

*Jesus answered, "How can the guests of the bride-
groom fast while he is with them? They cannot, so long as
they have him with them. But the time will come when the
bridegroom will be taken from them, and on that day they
will fast"* (Mark 2:18-20).

You see how marvelously consistent is the Word of God. In
case we were unsure whether Jesus was referring to Himself as a
Bridegroom when he spoke to the disciples in John chapter 14, we
find that at the very outset of their lives together Jesus had announced that He was the Bridegroom. So for three years, they had
known Him not only as rabbi and friend, but also the Bridegroom
with all of the inherent meaning which attended that word for those
of the Hebrew faith.

That is why Jesus did not need to fully explain His words about
leaving them. It was unnecessary for Him to once again tell them
He was the Bridegroom. They had had this understanding since the
first days when they began to follow Him. They knew Jesus was the
Bridegroom, that though He was with them there was coming a day
when He would leave them. That would be a day of fasting and
mourning. But as long as they were together, it was to be a time of
joy.

So, properly understood, the first verses of John 14 are not
really funeral verses at all. These words are all about a wedding, the
wedding of the Lord Jesus and His holy Bride. Let us spend the remainder of this chapter thinking about what that means to us as we
anticipate our role in that event that has been so long in coming.

It may seem strange at first to be thinking of first century marriage
customs to understand more about the return of Christ. But the ap-
propriateness of this is confirmed when we realize that God uses the

Jewish wedding to illustrate His plan of redemption and the unique relationship of Christ and His Bride, often called the Church.

In Old Testament days, the specifics of finding a wife for a young Jewish man varied a great deal, but there were a number of steps that seemed to be rather standard. First was that the initiative lay with the young man and his father. In the case of Jacob, he himself went to an area where his family ancestors still dwelt. There at the well in the fields, he met his wife-to-be Rachel, the daughter of his uncle Laban. While there he arranged to pay the price to her family to secure Rachel as his bride; he would work for her father for seven years (Genesis 29:1-18).

Earlier, Jacob's father Isaac had secured his wife from the same family, but instead of going himself to find her, his father Abraham sent a servant to do so. When he had met Rebekah at the bride's family well and was convinced by God that she was the proper person for his master's son to marry he quickly secured the blessings of Rebekah's father. "Then the servant brought out gold and silver jewelry and articles of clothing and gave them to Rebekah; he also gave costly gifts to her brother and to her mother" (Genesis 24:53). Thus, he paid the bride price.

In these two stories we see the first two steps in the Jewish marriage ritual: the selection of the bride-to-be and the payment of the bride price. When the price had been paid the marriage covenant was thereby established. They were betrothed, which carried a far greater commitment than our engagement period. Though no physical union had taken place, they were considered to be husband and wife.

Now, let us see how this applies to the Lord Jesus. This very issue of the betrothal came into play at the time of the birth of Jesus. His mother Mary was betrothed to Joseph. When she became pregnant by the Holy Spirit, it was a real crisis for Joseph. The Scripture says, "His mother Mary was pledged to be married to Joseph, but before they came together, she was found to be with child" (Matthew 1:18). This was a scandalous situation. The betrothal meant that she belonged to Joseph, but during this period they lived apart and had no sexual relationship. In a very real sense the two of them were married but awaiting the time of the consummation of their union.

In the very same way, Jesus left His Father's house and came to earth at the Father's command to provide salvation from sin and, those who would accept this wonderful offer would be granted the privilege of being a part of the Bride of Jesus. But for this to take place, before the wedding covenant could be announced, the bride price must be paid.

And Jesus paid the highest price possible. Through His sacrificial death on the cross and the shedding of His own blood, the price of redemption was paid. Now it was up to those who would believe and accept salvation to determine who would become the Bride of Christ. This was the greatest bride price ever paid and the Apostle Paul reminded the Corinthian Christians who were a part of the Bride to remember a very sobering fact: "You are not your own; you were bought at a price" (1 Corinthians 6:19b).

So, the bride having been selected and the bride price paid, the marriage covenant was established. She was set apart as his. She belonged to him. She became one who was set apart exclusively for her husband. The Bible uses a word to indicate when a person or thing is set apart for God's use. That powerful word is *sanctified*.

Those who are a part of the Bride of Christ are sanctified and are to be faithful to the Lord Jesus.

"The moment the covenant was established, the bride was declared to be set apart exclusively for the bridegroom. The groom and the bride then drank from a cup over which the betrothal benediction had been pronounced. This symbolized that the covenant relationship had been established." [12]

For Christians, Jesus did a very similar thing. In the upper room on the night before His death, He took a cup from the Passover table and drank from it with the disciples in an enactment of the betrothal ritual. As He did so, He spoke these words that have so much more meaning when we understand them in the context of the betrothal ceremony: "This is my blood of the covenant" (Mark 14:24).

How deeply significant is the Communion service when we understand the actions and words in light of the wedding covenant. One gospel writer records Jesus saying those words which have been carved into countless thousands of communion tables, "...do this in remembrance of me" (Luke 22:19) when we receive the bread and wine. That is one important aspect of the Lord's Supper: we look back at the sacrifice of Jesus by His broken body and shed blood.

But when we lift the cup to our lips we are not only looking back in remembrance, we are also looking forward. We are reaffirming our covenant with the heavenly Bridegroom until He comes for us. What a thrilling moment it is when we lift the cup and in so doing say I am waiting in expectancy as the Bride of Christ. It would be appropriate to say every time we receive the Communion cup those closing words of Revelation, "Amen. Come, Lord Jesus" (Revelation 22:20).

It is at this point that we return to that key passage at the beginning of John 14, "I am going there [to my Father's house] to prepare a place for you" (John 14:2). After the marriage covenant was in effect, the time came for the man to leave his bride and go to secure a place for them to live as husband and wife. This typically was at the home of the bridegroom's father. The custom was for a man about to be married to add a room or a small apartment onto the house of his father. Probably it had been the grandfather's house and the new bridegroom's father had built an addition when he was going to be bringing home his new wife.

Now the grandson would add on yet another dwelling. You can see the ruins of many of this type of extended family dwellings in Israel today. As the young man left his new bride at the home of her parents, he would speak words of encouragement and promise: "And if I go and prepare a place for you, I will come back and take you to be with me that you also may be where I am" (John 14:3).

Thus Jesus spoke those same words that night. He was going back to His Father's house and make all things ready for His Bride to be with Himself. The King James Version of the Bible says that in the Father's house are many mansions. I believe that the word "rooms," as used in the New International Version is probably a better one for us to use. Whatever size of place that Jesus prepares, it will be just right for the Bride of God's Son.

When a person visits the Vanderbilt family home named Biltmore in Asheville, North Caroline, one cannot help but be overwhelmed simply by its size. It has 250 rooms and is probably the largest family dwelling in the United States. But, child of God, rejoice! As the Bride of Christ we have something better and finer. "...we have a building from God, an eternal house in heaven, not built by human hands" (2 Corinthians 5:1). It is the place that at this present moment is being readied for the Bride's homecoming.

Those young Jewish fellows might take about a year to complete the work. Any period of time is a long time for a betrothed couple to wait for the consummation of their marriage. It is no different for the Bride of Christ. These nearly two thousand years have doomed forever for the waiting Bride. Some have given up and are no longer watching for His appearing. Others have let their zeal for the Bridegroom lag. Some have fallen into Satan's snare. Some have decided that He has already come back by His Holy Spirit so He is here now and we don't need to expect Him to come bodily. Others yet believe that there is no such thing as His return and that those who believe in that are a bunch of misguided zealots. If you were the Bridegroom, how would you feel if that were the kind of Bride to which you were expecting to return and claim to be with you forever.

To combat this lack of preparedness, Jesus sent a group of love letters to His Bride to help them be prepared and ready when He returns. We find these little notes in the Revelation in the second and third chapters. But to rightly understand them, we need to understand the full meaning of the Bride and the Bridegroom. Let us now look at the final steps in the Jewish wedding covenant.

While the groom is away preparing their living quarters in his father's house, the young Jewish bride is busy. The period of separation gives her ample time to prepare for married life and to select her wardrobe and fill her hope chest.

What is the Bride of Christ doing during His absence? Her primary responsibility is to make herself ready in purity, holiness and works of righteousness. The Bridegroom is praying for her. We find a wonderful promise in these words, "Christ Jesus, who died— more than that, who was raised to life—is at the right hand of God and is also interceding for us" (Romans 8:34). He is also building up the Bride through the work of the Holy Spirit in her. This work is carried on as members of the Body of Christ use their spiritual gifts to up-build each other as we read in Ephesians.

it was he [Jesus] who gave some to be apostles, some to be prophets, some to be evangelists, and some to be pastors and teachers, to prepare God's people for works of service so that the body [Bride] of Christ may be built up... (Ephesians 4:11,12).

So, this time of waiting is not just idle passing of time. It is to be an intensely vigorous and active time as the Bride readies herself with a watchful ear waiting to hear that the Bridegroom is coming at last.

In the Jewish tradition, at the end of the separation time, the groom along with his attendants leave the father's house and make their journey to the home of the bride. This will often take place at night and take the form of a torch-light procession. The Bride knew that He was coming, but never did she know when. She needed to be always prepared and be attuned to hear the shout, "Here's the bridegroom! Come out to meet him!" (Matthew 25:6).

This part of the wedding covenant tradition forms the most exciting part of the expectation of the snatching away of the Bride. This is often referred to as the Rapture. We find this glorious event detailed for us by Paul the apostle.

> *For the Lord himself will come down from heaven, with a loud command, with the voice of the archangel and with the trumpet call of God, and the dead in Christ will rise first. After that, we who are still alive and are left will be caught up with them in the clouds to meet the Lord in the air. And so we shall be with the Lord forever* (1 Thessalonians 4:16,17).

So the Groom receives his earthly bride and she goes with him to the place He has prepared. There they enter into the bridal chamber and have physical union for the first time, thus consummating the marriage.

The union of Jesus and His Bride will take place in heaven and it will be for all time. Together they will enjoy the matchless wonders of the heavenly kingdom for a period until they return together in the Glorious Appearing, which we often call the Second Coming, to bring the Tribulation to a swift conclusion. Then She will enjoy the responsibilities of being with her Husband when He takes His place upon the throne of David to begin His earthly reign that will last for one thousand years in the restored earth and after that for all eternity in the new heaven and the new earth.

There we have it! Those words from John 14:2, "I will come back," which are so innocuous to our non-Jewish ears take on a great wealth of meaning when we understand them in the same way as did they to whom they were first spoken. Those Jewish disciples would have immediately recognized that here were phrases from the wedding covenant and that Yeshua was establishing the same covenant with them

There are hundreds of promises in the Scriptures but certainly none is more tender, more powerful, more filled with hope, more bursting with excitement, than the promise made by the Bridegroom Jesus to His Bride just prior to His return to the Father's house. And because Jesus is the truth, we can be assured that indeed He will come and He will receive His Bride, just as He promised.

> *Jesus says:*
> *"Let not your hearts be troubled*
> *Because I said, 'I go away.'*
> *I'm going to my Father's house,*
> *But I'll come for you some day."*

> *Jesus says:*
> *"Let not your hearts be troubled;*
> *I'll prepare a place for you.*
> *Then I'll come and take you home*
> *With all the faithful and true."*

> *Jesus says:*
> *"Let not your hearts be troubled;*
> *I will not forget my Bride.*
> *Be ready, watching, waiting;*
> *You will soon be by my side."*

> *Jesus says:*
> *"Let not your hearts be troubled;*
> *Keep on working fruitfully.*
> *When you hear the trumpet's sound,*
> *You will know for sure it's me."*

Jesus says:
"Let not your hearts be troubled;
The Bridegroom will soon appear.
Have your lamps filled and burning
When I call out, 'Come up here.'"

Jesus says:
"Let not your hearts be troubled;
Preparation's almost done.
Heaven is standing on tip-toe
For the marriage of the Son"[13]

Study Three Notes

1. Ray Bachman. *The Love Letters of Jesus,* Morning Star Ministries, Mountain Home, AR, © 2010, pp. 9-63 (entire chapter).
2. Dan Brown, *The Da Vinci Code,* New York, NY, Doubleday, © 2003), p. 250.
3. Ibid., p. 244.
4. Ibid., p. 245
5. Margaret Starbird, *Mary Magdalene, Bride in Exile* (Rochester, VT, Bear and Co., © 2005, p. 88
6. Brown, op cit., p. 250
7. Starbird, op cit., p. 156
8. Joe Van Koevering, *Revealing the Da Vinci Code Deception,* St. Petersburg, FL, God's News Behind the News, © 2006, p. 82.
9. Kirk Talley, *Wedding Music,* (Kirk Talley Music/BMI)
10. Peter Jonsson Aschan, *O Let Your Soul Now Be Filled with Gladness,* Covenant Press, © 1972
11. Bill Gothard, *The Wedding Covenant,* Oak Brook, IL, Institute in Basic Youth Conflicts, © 1985
12. Ibid., p. 7.
13. Ray Bachman, *The Bridegroom's Promise,* Morning Star Ministries, Mountain Home, AR, , © 2008

Study Four

The Messiah in the Feasts of the Lord

How Jesus Fulfills the Feasts Commanded to Israel

As Christians begin to study Bible prophecy they are immediately confronted with the fact that they may have no real points of reference upon which to base their understanding. Thus, it is extremely easy to make some incorrect assumptions. One of these may be that it is Christians and the Church to which most prophecies in the Scriptures point.

And this assumption may well be under-girded by an unconscious grounding in the concept that the Christian Church has replaced the Jewish people as the the people of God. Many persons have unwittingly sat under the teaching of this insidious doctrine which is often known as Replacement Theology. If that is our understanding, we will soon discover that we wrongly interpret much of Bible Prophecy. That alone gives reason why so many persons who have an expressed desire to know more about the end times often soon come to the place of throwing up their hands in failure to make sense of the prophetic Scriptures. They begin their study journey with a faulty map and thus end their journey as lost in their understanding as before they started out.

What can we do to alleviate this problem? The primary concept we must grasp is that God desires for us to know and understand His plans and purposes for the end times, and He has put in His Word a great number of helps to bring that about. Primarily, of course, are the direct words of prophecy that are recorded throughout the Scriptures, both Old and New Testament. These are records of the exact words that God gave the prophetic writers to convey. Therefore, we need to take those words at their literal and face value, even if we don't fully understand them.

There is, however, an additional way in which the Lord God had chosen to reveal the future to us. That wonderful manner is comprised of teachings and events which are types and shadows of things to come. They have meanings in and of themselves, but they also point to future events with exciting clarity. One of these rich sources of information and meaning for us is found in the Feasts of God. They are often referred to as the Feasts of Israel, because God gave them to the Jewish people and they are the ones who have observed them for centuries and do so even today.

God has established an infinitely meaningful and profound prophetic system through His choices of seven holy convocations to be held each year by the Chosen People. He dictated the dates and proper observances to Moses on Mount Sinai, and His instructions are recorded in the crucial chapter of Leviticus 23. Zola Levitt emphasized the importance of this chapter.

> *It should be noted that God was very practical in issuing the seven feasts within one brief chapter of instruction. They are mentioned elsewhere in Scripture, but these vital and fundamental requirements of the Old Covenant were gathered together in simplest form lest no one overlook any of them.*[1]

Before we move on to examine these seven special annual events which God has ordained, we need to first clear away some misconceptions which may plague our comprehension. First of all is the word "feast." With our human desire to enjoy a tasty and enjoyable banquet, we must not think that the first and primary function of the special days is designed for a sumptious meal. Most of the seven events do have a meal as a part of their ritual, but that meal is quite secondary to the historical or spiritual meaning which God intends.

When, secondly, God speaks of these events, He more often than not refers to them as holy convocations. If we would think of them in that light, we will most likely then have a significant grasp on the purpose of these special days. Convocation literally means to be called together. That meaning is present in all of the seven convocations; they are not personal devotional days but ones of Israel celebrating together.

A third important concept to remember is that these feasts were given to the Jewish people. While they have significance for Christians, especially in understanding God's entire plan of redemption, they are not addressed to the followers of Jesus.

Remembering that all seven of these special events are for God's people, the Jews, will enable us to not only know God's plan for their redemption, but will help us to realize how Christian believers in Almighty God fit into His total plan. That the feasts are intended first and foremost for Israel is made quite clear in God's statement to Moses before the instructions for the special celebrations were given.

The Lord said to Moses, "Speak **to the Israelites** *and say to them; 'These are my appointed feasts, the appointed feasts of the Lord, which you are to proclaim as sacred assemblies'"* (Leviticus 23:1 emphasis added).

Fourthly, while all of these feasts or convocations have been in full operation since they were received through Moses from God, there is a most exciting aspect of study in them for us. As we look at the feasts we realize how they have had a Messianic fulfillment in some of them. This leads us to believe with confidence that the remaining feasts will likewise be fulfilled by *Yeshua ha Meshiach,* Jesus the Messiah. That truth forms the foundation of this study. We want to see more clearly how Jesus clearly and completely is discovered in these feasts which God has commanded. In so doing, we will be drawn ever closer to the realization that the truths of the Christian faith can not be well understood apart from a knowledge of God's covenant relationship with His Chosen People.

Another key component to our understanding of these annual festivals is found in the agrarian nature of Jewish life at the time God set forth these special days. Thus, we find that the feasts are all integrally related to the weather, rainfall and harvest. If we fail to keep this perspective, we can very well miss much of the inherent meaning and purpose for the celebrations. We will speak more of this essential aspect of God's intent.

Perhaps this is an appropriate point to set forth what I believe to be the proper attitude towards the observance of the feasts of God by Christians. There are those who teach that believers in Jesus as their Savior and also as the Jewish Messiah should begin to celebrate the feasts as fully as possible. There are others who would proclaim that since this is part of the Jewish law, that they were superseded by the sacrifice of Christ and are unworthy of much, if any, attention from Christians.

There is a better way to look at these very uniquely ordained events. They have a very special and practical message for the Jews that is both historical and prophetical. They each point to the promised Messiah of the Jews. We, as Christians, believe that looked-for Messiah to be the Lord Jesus Christ. Therefore, we can discover much of value to us, as we examine the deep meaning with which God has endued these ordinances. We need not make an attempt to keep the feasts in the sense with which the Jews are commanded to do. Neither do we dare fail to discover the great plan which God has revealed through them. Levitt has well stated this principle:

> *Believers in Christ are not responsible to keep these feasts, of course, but a knowledge of them greatly enhances their faith. The Lord kept every one of them without fail, even celebrating Passover on His last earthly night.*[2]

Another facet of the feasts that we must grasp before we look at the specific festivals is that of the terminology for Sabbath. Failure to understand what God says about His Sabbaths will cause us to have great difficulty in properly comprehending the meaning and timing of these designated days and events. For most of us non-Jews, when we hear the term Sabbath, we immediately think of the weekly day of worship. God carefully defined the weekly Sabbath:

> *There are six days when you may work, but the seventh day is a Sabbath of rest, a day of sacred assembly. You are not to do any work; wherever you live, it is a Sabbath to the Lord* (Leviticus 23:3).

Please note some important truths in this single verse. First, the Sabbath is the seventh day of the week. This is patterned after God's creation activity in which He made all that was created in six days and then proclaimed the seventh day as a day of rest. So, in our terminology of days which are named rather than numbered, the weekly Sabbath is always on Saturday. Because Christians worship on Sunday and often consider it a day of rest, especially in generations past, Sunday has often been referred to as the Sabbath day. This is incorrect. God designated the seventh day as the Sabbath and we would do well to keep that terminology intact as we study Bible prophecy. An appropriate term for Sunday is The Lord's Day in recognition of the resurrection of Jesus.

However, and this is where it can become confusing, God has also designated days other than the seventh day as Sabbaths. In the above verse, He gave an alternate term for the Sabbath, that of "sacred assembly." So, in the remainder of Leviticus 23 where He spells out the sacred feasts, God will often call for a day of sacred assembly, or as the King James Version calls them, "a holy convocation." These days of sacred assembly are also Sabbath days. The impact of this is that as we study the feasts we will find that

90

there are many more Sabbath days than we expect because they are not limited to the weekly seventh day.

The Names of the Feasts

Prior to our beginning to take a close-up look at each of them, let's become familiar with the names of the seven feasts which God has ordained for His people the Jews. I am also listing the name by which the feasts are often known in Hebrew as well as the month and day of the Hebrew calendar on which each feast begins. Don't worry about not understanding all of this right now. Begin to become familiar with the terms and manner of dating which we will look at individually.

Spring Feasts
1. Passover (Pesach) — Nisan 14
2. Unleavened Bread (Chag Hamotzi) — Nisan 15-22
3. First Fruits (Yom habikkurim) — Nisan 16

Summer Feast
4. Pentecost or Feast of Weeks (Shavu'ot) — Sivan 6

Fall Feasts
5. Trumpets (Yom Teru'ah) — Tishri 1
6. Atonement (Yom Kippur) — Tishri 10
7. Tabernacles (Sukkot) — Tishri 15

Not everyone groups the seven feasts in the same way. I prefer the above grouping because of the harvest factor involved in each group. God is concerned for a bountiful harvest of souls and He has structured His annual pattern of worship for his people around the three harvest seasons which are so important for this agriculturally oriented society. The Feast of First Fruits in the spring commemorates the barley harvest. The summer wheat harvest is the focal point of the Feast of Weeks while the fall feasts are planned to coincide with the olive and grape harvests. We will see later how each of these are to remind God's people of His deliverance.

Chapter 23 of Leviticus is one of the most significant portions of Scripture in the entire Bible. God lays out a plan for the Hebrew people and commands them to carefully observe it. And it is of utmost importance that we realize that these sacred observances have deep, profound meaning for Christians as well as the Israelites. Scott McAllister has well stated this connection.

> *Each feast represents a prophetic sign concerning the life and ministry of the Lord Jesus Christ. These signs apply, consequently, also to the Church, the Body of Christ. The entire plan of God for humanity is, in an extraordinary manner, revealed by the nature and exact dates of the seven feasts of the LORD that the Israelites were to observe. The entire destiny of the human race unfolds between the first and the last feast.*[3]

We should note at this point there there are other festival celebrations that are important to the Jewish people. Those of Hanukkah, or the Feast of Dedication, and Purim, the Feast of Esther, are two principal ones with which we are most familiar. While these are very significant, they are later additions and are not among those given by God on Mount Sinai to Moses. We may say a word about them later, but our primary emphasis shall be on the seven sacred assemblies commanded by God.

With this brief introduction, let us now proceed to examine more fully each of the seven special observances that God has commanded for His people Israel and see as well the marvelous prophetic outline contained within them. By so doing, we will discover that there is a deeply rooted connection between the Jewish and Christian followers of Jehovah that is seldom proclaimed in either of these two great faiths. As we draw increasingly closer to the events of the End Times, a careful examination of the Feasts of the Lord will enable us to be more cognizant of God's great plan and how He is soon bringing it to its final fulness in the Messiah, His Son, Jesus Christ.

The Spring Feasts

We examine the three spring feasts as a unit as they are inextricably bound together both by meaning and by dating. Passover, Unleavened Bread and First Fruits are part and parcel of one another. In fact, they are so closely related that the entire week in which they occur is often called by either the single name of Passover or Unleavened Bread to refer to the total eight days encompassed by the three feasts.

Only a few words command the feast of Passover in Leviticus 23. God says simply, "The Lord's Passover begins at twilight on the fourteenth day of the first month" (Leviticus 232:5). The reason He did not speak more detail was that this feast was already firmly in mind by the Hebrews for God had given them the precise plan for the first feast while still in Egypt. We find those details to read thus:

93

> *This month is to be for you the first month, the first month of your year. Tell the whole community of Israel that on the tenth day of this month each man is to take a lamb for his family, one for each household. . . .Take care of them until the fourteenth day of the month, when all the people of the community of Israel must slaughter them at twilight. Then they are to take some of the blood and put it on the sides and tops of the doorframes of the houses where they eat the lambs. . . .On that same night I will pass through Egypt and strike down every firstborn—both men and animals—and I will bring judgment on all the gods of Egypt; I am the Lord. The blood will be a sign for you on the houses where you are; and when I see the blood, I will pass over you. No destructive plague will touch you when I strike Egypt.*
>
> *This is a day you are to commemorate; for the generations to come you shall celebrate it as a festival to the Lord—a lasting ordinance* (Exodus 12:1-3, 6-7, 12-14).

It is certainly not by accident that Passover is the first of the seven feasts God commanded for the Jewish people. It is basic and foundational for all that God has planned for man. His deliverance of the Hebrew people from the Egyptians is indicative of the very nature and heart of God. He desires to deliver His people. Passover is not just a commemorative event celebrating an event in Egypt; it is a pattern for God's relationship to man. This truth is so well stated by Mark Levitt and quoted by John Parsons:

> *Passover is the Feast of Salvation. In both testaments, the blood of the Lamb delivers from slavery—the Jew from Egypt, the Christian from sin. . . .Jesus serves as the sacrificial lamb. It is no coincidence that our Lord Himself was sacrificed on Passover. In Egypt the Jew marked his house with the blood of the lamb. Today the Christian marks his house—his body, "the house of the spirit" with*

94

the blood of Christ. Passover, then represents our salvation[4]

In the passage from Exodus 12, we note that God commanded the month in which the original Passover took place to become the first month of the year for the Hebrew people. That month today is known on the Jewish calendar as Nisan. This means that the Jewish sacred year begins in the spring at the time of the barley harvest in Israel. All months on the Jewish calendar begin with the new moon. It is essential that we grasp a bit of how Jewish time was reckoned if we are to understand either Jewish history or Bible prophecy. It is always related to the Jewish calendar and not to the one we are accustomed to using.

In the same regard, we must continually remind ourselves that the Jewish day in the Bible begins not at midnight, as is our custom. Their day commences at twilight or sundown. Thus, when we see on our calendar that Passover, for instance, is on a Tuesday, we must remember that the feast day actually starts at sundown on Monday. It takes some getting used to, but we must do so to grasp the reality of what we read. Thus, when it is stated that something happens at twilight, it is not referring to the end of the day, but to its beginning. This truth is evident from the very beginning. After each day of creation the Scripture says, "And there was evening, and there was morning." This concept is crucial as we read what happened in the days of Passover and Unleavened Bread during the final week in the life of Jesus.

Another thing for which to watch to avoid confusion is the way both the Bible and the Jewish people often refer to the feast days. Passover, Unleavened Bread and First Fruits all occur within an eight day period, with the first day correctly being known as Passover with the seven days of Unleavened Bread beginning the following day. However, we will often see reference to "the first day of Passover" which indicates they are referring to the entire period of the Spring feasts. Likewise, it is often spoken of as "the first day of Unleavened Bread" and is meant to include Passover. So we must be vigilant to note the context which will usually enable us to identify just what day is being meant.

So let's get in mind the time-line of the Spring feasts. The Passover lamb was to be selected on the tenth day of Nisan (Exodus 12:3) and to be watched and cared for until the day it would be killed which was on Nisan 14, Passover Day. The seven days of Feast of Unleavened Bread began on the following day, Nisan 15. Somewhere during that week would be the regular weekly Sabbath on the seventh day of the week. The Feast of First Fruits occurred on the day following the regular Sabbath, so First Fruits would always take place on the first day of the week, while Passover could occur on any day of the week depending on the date of the full moon.

To quickly summarize the intended meaning of the spring feasts for the Jews, we see there are at least three great messages. First of all, Passover is a remembrance of the experience of deliverance of the Hebrews from Egypt. They were saved from the final plague of the death of every firstborn by the blood of the sacrificial lamb which had been smeared on the doorposts and lintel of their homes. When God saw the blood, He did as He promised, "I will pass over you" (Exodus 13). So Passover is both remembrance and representation of the deliverance from bondage in Egypt.

In Leviticus 23, God gives only very brief words commanding the continuing observance of Passover. This brevity is possible only because God gave lengthy and comprehensive instructions for Passover and Unleavened Bread which are recorded in Exodus 12. It would be helpful in your understanding if you would read that entire chapter before continuing in your reading of this book.

The second aspect of the Spring feasts is Unleavened Bread. The Hebrews were to leave Egypt in a hurry without time for bread to rise from the use of leavening. Yeast in Scripture is symbolic of sin in the life of God's people. So God was giving a living picture of His expectation; after their deliverance His people were to live above sin in their lives. As a week-long feast, Unleavened Bread is a reminder that a life of holiness was not a feast day observance but that which was to take place every day of the week.

Thirdly, First Fruits emphasizes God's provision of harvest. The barley harvest took place in the spring and reminded God's people of their dependence upon God's faithfulness. They were to celebrate the fertility of the land which God had given them by bringing sheaves of the very first of the harvest and to wave them before the Lord as a "wave offering" of thanksgiving in anticipation of a full and bountiful harvest.

So, those in summary are the Spring feasts and their background. But there is far more. Not only were these feast days grounded in the experience of God with Israel, but they are packed with meaning of God's gracious plan of redemption for all persons. Thus, we need to see how these feasts find a fulfillment in the Lord Jesus Christ, Israel's Messiah.

Passover is quite obvious. Jesus Himself used the week of celebration beginning with Passover to show forth the marvelous plan of redemption which He put in play during his final week on earth. He came into the holy city, Jerusalem, on Nisan 10, identifying Himself as the Passover lamb. He chose to eat the Passover Seder with His disciples as His final meal with them. His death on the Roman cross on Passover was the opening of the way of salvation for all who would put their faith in Him and receive the offer of deliverance and redemption from sin. He demonstrated this in the salvation of the repentant thief on a cross adjoining His own.

The burial of Jesus at the beginning of Unleavened Bread was a powerful symbol of the putting away of sin. Just as the Hebrew people cleansed their homes from everything containing yeast as a symbol of uncleanness, so Jesus took the power of sin and death with Him to the grave. When He came forth from the grave, it was on the morning of First Fruits. He was the beginning of a bountiful harvest of souls whom God would bring forth with deliverance from the power of sin to live a life of holiness.

So, while we do not, according to Scripture, need to observe these feasts, we must of necessity be aware of the deep spiritual attachment which is present between the followers of Jesus and the feasts of Israel. When we see this connection we are more fully aware of both our heritage and our debt to Judaism. God's plan of salvation is consistent from the beginning. He set the feasts in place to help all men see that there is no deliverance from the bondage of sin apart from His Messiah whose name is Yeshua.

The Summer Feast

While we see three contiguous feasts in the spring, there is one feast that stands alone in the summer. That is the Feast of Weeks or as Christians commonly know it, Pentecost. The term comes from the Greek word *pente* which means fifty. Pentecost is fifty days after First Fruits. For this reason, in the minds of many scholars it is very often linked to the spring feasts.

We find the formula for dating Pentecost in Leviticus 23:15, 16. "From the day after the Sabbath, the day you brought the sheaf of the wave offering [First Fruits], count off seven full weeks. Count off fifty days up to the day after the seventh Sabbath, and then present an offering of new grain to the Lord." Since it occurs on the day after the seventh Sabbath, Pentecost will always fall on the first day of the week, or Sunday. It is an additional Sabbath.

The festival occurs at the time of the wheat harvest, in contrast with First Fruits which celebrated the barley harvest. However, the instructions for Pentecost are not for a wave offering of grain, but for the presentation of two loaves of bread made from the new grain. "From wherever you live, bring two loaves made of two-tenths of an ephah of fine flour, baked with yeast, as a wave offering of firstfruits to the Lord" (Leviticus 23:17). Zola Levitt has a most interesting commentary on this verse which enables us again to see the Christian-Jewish connection.

This subtle instruction indicates a great truth. These two "wave loaves" are of equal weight and they are baked with leaven. They are called "firstfruits." Since they are baked with leaven, they represent sinful man (certainly not, for example, Jesus and the Holy Spirit who are unleavened) and since they are "firstfruits" they are redeemed or resurrected men. Obviously God was predicting here that the Church would be comprised of two parts, Jew and Gentile. We seem to think of the Church today as entirely Gentile, but of course it has always been part Jewish, since the Lord inevitably retains a remnant of His people. The greater body of Jews will join the Church in the kingdom at the Second Coming (Zechariah 12:10; 13:1) when "All Israel will be saved" (Romans 11:26).[5]

As God used the annual Feast of Weeks to remind the people of His provision for an abundant grain harvest, He gave the festival an even greater emphasis on harvest on the day in which the awaiting disciples of Yeshua received the outpouring of the Holy Spirit on the Day of Pentecost just fifty days after His resurrection. The harvest that day was a harvest of souls numbering 3,000 and ushered in the age of the Christian Church which would be engaged in the harvest of men for the Savior until He comes to claim Her as His Bride.

It is noteworthy that the initial harvest was comprised largely of Jewish souls present in Jerusalem for the day of Pentecost. For almost two millenia this harvest of Jews and Gentiles has been taking place under the anointing of the Holy Spirit just as Jesus indicated only ten short days before the feast and as His final words before ascending to the Father.

But you will receive power when the Holy Spirit comes on you; and you will be my witnesses in Jerusalem, and in all Judea and Samaria, and to the ends of the earth (Acts 1:8).

And so, while Israel still celebrates the Feast of Pentecost as an annual festival, the Church of Jesus lives out Pentecost on a daily basis. As individual believers receive the Holy Spirit and appropriate His power for witness, the reaping of the harvest continues. Indeed, in terms of prophetic fulfillment of the Feasts of God, we now stand between the fourth and fifth of these solemn convocations, as they are called by the Lord.

This calls for a review of the first four feasts. Pesach or Passover was fulfilled by the death of Jesus as a symbol of salvation and redemption. His burial fulfilled Unleavened Bread as the evidence of the putting away of sin. His resurrection on First Fruits gloriously fulfilled the feast by becoming the first of millions who would experience resurrection from the grave through faith in Him. And on the Day of Pentecost or Shavu'ot, He inaugurated the great spiritual harvest through the empowering of the Holy Spirit that continues until today.

Since these first four feasts of the Jewish year have found a perfect fulfillment through Jesus the Messiah, can we not expect that He will also bring fulfillment to the final three? As exciting as it is to realize what God has done through Jesus on these four feasts, it is even more thrilling to contemplate what God has in store for His people on the final celebrations, those of the fall season.

The Pilgrim Feasts

Before beginning our look at the three fall feasts, we might well break in at this point and say a word about the pilgrim feasts, or the feasts that require a pilgrimage to Jerusalem. While the feasts are to

CHRISTIANS, JEWS and the END TIMES

be observed by all and are usually held in the homes of Jews wherever they are, yet the focus of the sacrifices was always at the Temple in Jerusalem. Thus, God commanded that during each of the three feast seasons that the men were to come up before the Lord at the Temple and make their sacrifices there. Notice God's plan for this in this abbreviated portion of Scripture.

> *Three times a year you are to celebrate a festival to me. Celebrate the Feast of Unleavened Bread. . .No one is to appear before me empty-handed. Celebrate the Feast of Harvest [Pentecost] with the firstfruits of the crops you sow in your field. Celebrate the Feast of Ingathering [Tabernacles] at the end of the year when you gather in your crops from the field. Three times a year all the men are to appear before the Sovereign Lord (Exodus 23:14-17).*

Alfred Kolatch explains the purpose of these pilgrimages.

> *In the Jewish calendar Pesach, Shavuot and Sukkot are referred to as "Pilgrim Festivals" because on these holidays all men were required to make a pilgrimage to the Temple in Jerusalem (Exodus 23:17). All three were originally agricultural holidays, and in celebration of them the Jews of Palestine brought the first crops of the season to the Temple, where a portion was offered as a sacrifice and the balance used by the Priestly families. Only after this obligation was fulfilled were the new season's crops permitted to be used as food.[6]*

I make mention of the required pilgrimages, not because they have great significance in and of themselves, but because they demonstrate to us how important is Jerusalem and the Temple in God's eyes. He, of course, is omnipresent. We don't have to journey to a particular place to meet Him. However, God has chosen to select a specific place to focus our attention on His actions. This is especially true as we study the final three feasts and notice how they center for their fulfillment around Jerusalem, the Temple mount and the surrounding area. Listen to the passionate words which God declares in reference to Jerusalem:

> This is what the Lord Almighty says: "I am very jealous for Zion; I am burning with jealousy for her." This is what the Lord says: "I will return to Zion and dwell in Jerusalem. Then Jerusalem will be called the City of Truth, and the mountain of the Lord Almighty will be called the Holy Mountain" (Zechariah 8:2-3).

As Christians, we can come to more fully realize the importance of the Jewish roots of our faith if we can begin to sense and realize how important is Jerusalem in God's scheme of things for the end times. This is easier for those who have visited the Holy Land and walked the ancient streets of Jerusalem, stood in awe of her magnificent gates and marveled at the massive walls that surround this city which God calls His home.

If you have not been privileged to visit that place, read your Bible with a careful emphasis on the location that has stood as the capital of the Jewish people for over 3,500 years. God will begin to implant within your spirit a love and a longing for the city of the Great King.

Great is the Lord, and greatly to be praised in the city of our God, in the mountain of his holiness. Beautiful for situation, the joy of the whole earth, is Mount Zion, on the sides of the north, the city of the great King (Psalm 48:1f , KJV).

I also mention the city in the context of the feasts because there is no longer animal sacrifice on the Temple mount since no Temple has stood there since 70 A.D. This has caused the Jewish people to alter the way in which they celebrate some of the feasts. For instance, they no longer eat lamb at Passover since there are no lambs now sacrificed at the Temple. For Christians there might be a different attitude since they realize that the Lamb of God was slain once for all and that the annual sacrifice is no longer needed as an atonement for sin.

The feasts are not a static celebration for the Jews with strict adherence to the original form of the observance. Rather, they are dynamic celebrations whose style and meanings have evolved over these many centuries since they were originally received from God. Thus, we witness a wide diversity in the manner in which various Jewish groups celebrate the feasts today.

The Autumn Feasts

Just as there are three feasts clustered in the spring, so we see a similar grouping in the autumn feasts. These three are Trumpets or Rosh Hashanah, Yom Kippur or Day of Atonement and Tabernacles or Succoth. While in the first four feasts we are able to observe not only the original meaning for the Jews but also the fulfillment in Jesus the Messiah, we have a different perspective in the fall celebrations. In these final three we still see the inherent meaning for the Jewish celebration, but now we look in anticipation to how these will find their ultimate meaning in Yeshua sometime in the future.

What are the reasons and purposes for the autumn feasts? Sometimes these are a bit vague and at other times are extremely explicit. For instance when God calls for the feast of Trumpets, He says quite simply, "On the first day of the seventh month you are to have a day of rest, a sacred assembly commemorated with trumpet blasts" (Leviticus 23:24). We find instructions for the preparation and offering of sacrifices for that day in Numbers 29:1-6. God also makes the statement there that "It is a day for you to sound the trumpets" (vs. 1).

Over these many years, the Hebrews have added many other meanings to this day. Since Trumpets falls on the first day of the seventh month called Tishri in the religious calendar, it is the only feast day which begins on a new moon instead of a full moon. God has said that the seventh month would be the first month of the year. But Israel has two calendars. The second is the civil calendar and on the civil calendar Tishri is the first month of the year. So it is necessary that we keep this distinction in mind lest we become unnecessarily confused. On the religious calendar, Tishri, the seventh month, is to the year what the Sabbath is to the week, a period of rest. As the first month of the new civil year, it is also observed as Rosh Hashanah.

Since it is celebrated as the first day of the first month of the year on the civil calendar, it has come to have additional meanings.

A primary one is the celebration of creation, so it becomes a time of sacrifice and praise to God for His handiwork. Trumpets always play a major role in Scripture both in praising God and calling people to their proper place, calling to battle, calling to repentance and announcing major events. Since there were no printed calendars, trumpets were used to signal the beginning of a new month and were sounded additional times at the start of a new year. There is much more we could say about the Feast of Trumpets, but those are some of the key things for us to keep in mind.

The purpose of the Day of Atonement, called *Yom Kippur* in modern days, is quite evident. It was the day when sacrifice was made for the sins of the people as the High Priest went into the Holy of Holies only on that day in the entire year to spread the blood on the mercy seat, the cover of the Ark of the Covenant. This is a key day as it symbolizes that God has woven into the entire structure of the feasts His gracious plan of redemption. Tabernacles is the final feast of the autumn series and is the one which will continue throughout eternity as God tabernacles among His people in the person of the Lord Jesus.

As we saw in the spring feasts, the three fall feasts are linked together both by purpose and by their placement on the calendar. As we noted, Trumpets begins on the first day of the month of Tishri (Leviticus 23:24). The Day of Atonement comes nine days later on Tishri 10 (Leviticus 23:27) with the week long celebration of Tabernacles beginning on Tishri 15 (Leviticus 23:34). While these are three separate feasts, yet there is a continuity that is apparent and which must not be lost as we look in anticipation of how we expect to see these feasts fulfilled by Messiah in the future.

At this point it is imperative that we note that there is a significant disparity among prophecy teachers about the role of the Feast of Trumpets in terms of future expectations. There are many who hold to the position that the Rapture of the Bride of Christ will occur on the celebration of Trumpets, especially noting the fact that the Apostle Paul declares, "For the Lord himself will come down from heaven, with a loud command, with the voice of the archangel and with the trumpet call of God" (1 Thessalonians 4:16). There are many other Scriptures which are used to seemingly indicate that this is a logical and Biblically sound interpretation.

I used to believe that this was a most convenient way to put together God's prophetic message in the feasts He gave to teach His salvation plan, both for the Jews and the nations. But after more careful scrutiny of the Scriptures, I have realized that this is not a viable interpretation. I have at least four reasons for this view.

The first is that we must remember for whom the feasts of God were designed. They are for the Jews. In our enthusiasm to see Jesus in these feasts and in our own view of our importance as Christians, it is quite easy to get off-track at this point. There is not a single feast designated as for the Church. While we may have a rather direct connection to the fulfillment, we must interpret the feasts and their fulfillment in light of God's plan for the Jewish people.

A second reason to reject Trumpets as a date for the Rapture is the words of Jesus Himself. In responding to the disciple's question about the end of the age, Jesus gave words so important that He repeated them over and over. "No one knows about that day or hour. . .Therefore keep watch, because you do not know on what day your Lord will come. . . .the Son of Man will come at an hour when you do not expect him. . . .Therefore keep watch, because you do not know the day or the hour" (Matthew 24: 36, 42, 44, 25:13). If Jesus is to come for believers on the day of the Feast of Trumpets, then contrary to the words of Jesus, we would know the day.

A third thing to consider in this regard is that of the trumpet sound. Paul's quotation above indicated that the Rapture would take place at the sound of the trumpet of God. Others have related the Rapture with the last of the seven trumpets in Revelation chapter eight through eleven. However, those trumpets are sounded by seven angels (Revelation 9:6) not God Himself; neither are the trumpets which are sounded on the feast days. Those trumpets are the shofars made from animal horns which are sounded by men in Jerusalem to announce the time of the feasts.

Therefore, the Rapture is an imminent, stand-alone event that God Himself will announce with a trumpet blast that will be heard only by those who are being gathered together unto the Lord Jesus. It will be at an unknown moment which could be at any time, any day. The question of what is believed about the issue of imminence, or the any moment possible appearing of Christ as the Bridegroom, is a key factor in deciding how other End Time prophecies are perceived and understood.

A fourth and very significant reason to not equate the feast of Trumpets with the Rapture is the consistent nature of the Lord God. It is quite evident that the final two feasts, Day of Atonement and Tabernacles will not be fulfilled until the Second Coming of Messiah. To pull out the fulfillment of Trumpets and see it fulfilled apart from Atonement and Tabernacles would appear to run counter to the way God has designed His feasts. Just as the spring feasts flow together in meaning, purpose and timing, so do the trio of holy convocations which occur in the fall.

So, I conclude that it is best to see these feasts in concord, fulfilled in a single year and portraying to us God's final concluding plan of salvation for His people, the Jews. The Rapture, since it is an imminent event, may occur on the Feast of Trumpets, but it is highly unlikely that it will be the one at the conclusion of the Tribulation. Having said that, let us take a brief look at the meaning of each of these great solemn assemblies.

The instruction for the Feast of Trumpets is concise in the Leviticus listing: "The Lord said to Moses, 'Say to the Israelites: 'On the first day of the seventh month you are to have a day of rest, a sacred assembly commemorated with trumpet blasts. Do no regular work, but present an offering made to the Lord by fire'''" (Leviticus 23:23-25). If we had no other instructions for the day, it would appear to be little more than an additional Sabbath day. That is not the case, however. There are a great number of meanings that we need to note briefly to more fully understand this very important feast day.

The first day of the seventh month, Tishri, is the day observed as New Year's Day. We hear it referred to in our day as Rosh Hashanah. This may be confusing as we have already noted that the first day of Nisan is designated by God, "This month is to be the first month of your year" (Exodus 12:2). How do we reconcile these seemingly conflicting statements? Nisan is the beginning of the Jewish religious year which is based on God's deliverance from Egypt. Tishri is the beginning of the civil calendar which is based on God's creation.

As the seventh month of the year, it is a symbolic sabbath month and therefore designated as a day of rest, reflecting upon God's rest after the six day's of creation. We must be careful to search out the reason for Biblical statements which seem contradictory and difficult for us to understand.

Just as we often make resolutions at New Year's based on our self evaluation, so the Feast of Trumpets is a day for spiritual self examination and the beginning of a season of repentance which lasts for the ten days until the Day of Atonement on Tishri 10. Therefore, the sound of the trumpet is a call for the Hebrews to leave their daily routine and enter into a time of repentance in preparation for the Day of Atonement. Buksbazen has explained it, thus:

> *They are given ten days of repentance which are called Yomin Noraim, which means the fearsome or awesome days. During that period depending on the sincerity of their repentance, the Lord will judge them on the Day of Atonement.*
>
> *Since, according to popular Jewish belief, the majority of mankind are neither utterly good nor utterly wicked , the ten days are of the utmost importance. Much therefore depends on the behavior and repentance of the Jew during these "Ten Awesome Days."* [7]

How, therefore, do we see the ultimate fulfillment of this feast? Since, the 100 blasts of the trumpet was a call to leave their place of work and come together for a period of introspection and repentance, we need to seek our answer in what the prophetic writers tell us that could apply to this specific feast.

God said through Joel, "Blow the trumpet in Zion; sound the alarm on my holy hill. Let all who live in the land tremble, for the day of the Lord is coming. It is close at hand," and "Blow the trumpet in Zion, declare a holy fast, call a sacred assembly" (Joel 2:1, 15). This is helpful because it places the coming Feast of Trumpets to be fulfilled at the end of the Tribulation period as the term the "the day of the Lord" would indicate. Zechariah is referring to the same time as "on the day" when God has him proclaim,

> *And I will pour out on the house of David and the inhabitants of Jerusalem a spirit of grace and supplication. They will look on me, the one they have pierced, and they will mourn for him as one mourns for an only child, and grieve bitterly for him as one grieves for a first-born son"* (Zechariah 12:10).

Surely, this description could fit with the Feast of Trumpets at the end of the Tribulation.

The very first chapter of Revelation picks up these same words, thus setting the stage for the return of *Yeshua ha Mashiach* on the Feast of Trumpets to end the Tribulation. "Look, he is coming with the clouds, and every eye will see him, even those who pierced him; and all the peoples of the earth will mourn because of him. So shall it be! Amen" (Revelation 1:7).

Just as the Feast of Trumpets has always been a call to leave the place of labor and come before the Lord in a spirit of repentance, so on the final gathering for that feast will be a call to come and prepare to meet the Lord. Jesus Himself will be sending out the call for the remnant to return and to prepare for receiving their salvation. Notice how the words of Jesus in the Olivet Discourse parallel those quoted above from Revelation.

"At that time the sign of the Son of Man will appear in the sky, and all the nations of the earth will mourn. They will see the Son of Man coming on the clouds of the sky, with power and great glory. And he will send his angels with a loud trumpet call, and they will gather his elect from the four winds, from one end of the heavens to the other" (Matthew 24:30f).

This perfectly parallels the prophecy of Isaiah where God says: "He will raise a banner for the nations and gather the exiles of Israel; he will assemble the scattered people of Judah from the four quarters of the earth" (Isaiah 11:12). God has allotted ten days for this gathering, the mourning and repentance to take place before the second of the fall feasts.

The Lord said to Moses, "The tenth day of this seventh month is the Day of Atonement. Hold a sacred assembly and deny yourselves, and present an offering made to the Lord by fire. Do no work on that day, because it is the Day of Atonement, when atonement is made for you before the Lord your God" (Leviticus 23:26-28).

Throughout the hundreds of generations since Moses received this command from God for the Hebrew people, the Day of Atonement has been the most sacred and solemn day of the year for the Jewish people. It remains so today, no matter where they live on the earth. They have longed in their spirits for a time when they know they have been released from the bondage of their sin even as they were freed from the captivity of slavery in Egypt. But the atonement they were given has always been a temporary one with the necessity of returning to the same impotent ritual year after year. One writer has expressed this sad truth so well:

> *In spite of Yom Kippur, the day dedicated to atonement, there is no assurance of sins forgiven in Judaism. There is longing, there is hope for forgiveness, but of assurance, there is none. This only the Son of God can give to those who come to Him in faith. The Day of Atonement is only a substitute for Atonement.*
>
> *Deep in her heart Israel knows that her atonement is of the Messiah. He alone is able to bring forgiveness.*[8]

Zola Levitt reminds us again of how important it is to keep a Jewish perspective on the feasts. "But these are Jewish feasts, and each one is fulfilled for the Jews. The Day of Atonement will be fulfilled in a wonderful way when the Lord returns at His second coming."[9]

We read in the New Testament, "But these sacrifices are an annual reminder of sins, because it is impossible for the blood of bulls and goats to take away sins" (Hebrews 10:4f). But the ultimate fulfillment of the Day of Atonement will come on that day when the surviving remnant of Israel will find full and final atonement in the blood of Jesus.

> *The blood of goats and bulls and the ashes of a heifer sprinkled on those who are ceremonially unclean sanctify them so that they are outwardly clean. How much more, then, will the blood of Christ, who through the eternal Spirit offered himself unblemished to God, cleanse our consciences from acts that lead to death, so that we may serve the living God! For this reason Christ is the mediator*

of a new covenant, that those who are called may receive the promised eternal inheritance (Hebrews 9:13-15a).

It almost goes without saying that the event stated with certainty by the Apostle Paul will take place on the Day of Atonement which follows ten days after the Feast of Trumpets when Jesus comes in power and glory to gather the remnant of the Jewish people unto Himself, "And so all Israel will be saved, as it is written, 'The deliverer will come from Zion; he will turn godlessness away from Jacob. And this is my covenant with them when I take away their sins'" (Romans 11:26f).

The Jewish people will find on that final Day of Atonement the wonderful blessing of coming to that fountain filled with blood drawn from Immanuel's veins, for "On that day a fountain will be opened to the house of David and the inhabitants of Jerusalem, to cleanse them from sin and impurity" (Zechariah 13:1).

With the first two of the fall feasts finding fulfillment in Yeshua at the end of the Tribulation, can we not then with certainty know that the third feast will also be completed in due order. We are again given precise timing for this seventh feast.

"The Lord said to Moses, 'Say to the Israelites: 'On the fifteenth day of the seventh month the Lord's Feast of Tabernacles begins, and it lasts for seven days. The first day is a sacred assembly; do no regular work. For seven days present offerings made to the Lord by fire, and on the eighth day hold a sacred assembly and present an offering made to the Lord by fire. It is the closing assembly; do no regular work'" (Leviticus 23:33-36).

Rabbi Kolatch gives a good summary of the reason behind Tabernacles:

> *Although Sukkot was originally an agricultural holiday like Passover and Shavuot, the Bible (Leviticus 23:42-43) ascribes historical significance to it by stating its purpose: "You shall live in booths seven days in order that future generations may know that I made the Israelite people live in booths when I brought them out of the land of Egypt, I am the Lord your God." The sukkot (booths) that Jews build today are reminders of that forty-year sojourn in the desert on the way to the Promised Land.*[10]

Thus, the picture of the past reminding the Jews of the presence and help of God during their forty years in the wilderness is a shadow of the fact that Messiah will live and rule among His people after His second coming. Obviously, the Feast of Booths indicates how God is a shelter for His people. But, there is also the sense of "living with" inherent in the word tabernacle. The Tabernacle in the wilderness was not only a place of worship but a symbol of God dwelling in the midst of His people as they lived in the small huts or little tabernacles surrounding the Tabernacle of God who was dwelling with them and meeting their needs.

What a picture of what will take place after the inauguration of the Messianic Kingdom which will certainly take place on the seventh and final of the feasts given by God for His people. From that day forward, God's Messiah for Isaiah, and through them all the peoples of the world, will be dwelling personally in the midst of His people. He will establish His kingdom reign from Jerusalem. He will rule from the throne of David. He will establish justice and righteousness over the entire world. All people everywhere can come under the protection of the tabernacle established by Yeshua Himself.

And God indicates that this final feast is one to be observed throughout the entire thousand years of the Messianic reign. It is so important to Him that He is going to require every nation to send people annually to Jerusalem to celebrate the Fest of Tabernacles with the Jews who have done so for 3,500 years. He says, "Then the survivors from all the nations that have attacked Jerusalem will go up year after year to worship the King, the Lord Almighty, and to celebrate the feast of Tabernacles.

"If any of the peoples of the earth do not go up to Jerusalem to worship the King, the Lord Almighty, they will have no rain" (Zechariah 14:16f). And, thus, this solemn assembly will live up to another of its names, that of the Feast of Ingathering. The King Himself will gather the world around and tabernacle with them, this time not in the wilderness, but in the paradise of His Kingdom.

Conclusion

While there are a number of other highly significant feasts which the Jewish people celebrate on an annual basis, these seven are those which are properly called the Feasts of God. They are often referred to as the feasts of Israel; however, we must keep in mind that they are solemn assemblies which God has ordained and commanded for Israel. They are still for Israel. While we have an increasingly growing interest in them as Christians due to the fulfillment we see Christ Jesus bringing to each of them, it is

116

essential that we not lose sight of the fact that God gave them to the Jews.

The greatest and most exciting completion we will witness will be the day when the Jewish people are at last discovering for themselves their Messiah and receiving Him in faith. Then, during the Kingdom reign of the Lion of Judah, we will be united with them in serving Messiah and worshiping Him together during the Feast of Tabernacles.

At this point it might be helpful for us to hear a viewpoint from one approaching the subject with quite a different perspective. Rabbi Sandmel has written a rather large volume on the entire New Testament. He has an analysis of the topics we have been discussing which is pertinent to our own understanding as we Christians seek to foster a new and deeper relationship with our Jewish roots.

> *A summary may here be useful of the distance which early Christianity has traveled from its inherited Judaism even in the early age of Paul, as led by him. What it has carried over is the Jewish Scripture, though interpreted now in a new and unique way. It has a continued belief in the God of Israel and a sense of a special place in the divine scheme of things for Israel—except that Israel is no longer the Jewish people, but is instead the emerging Christian church.*
>
> *The rejection of the law of Moses implies an end to those two items most readily characterizing the usual Judaism. One of these is the dietary laws. The second is the religious calendar, with the New Year and the Day of Atonement in the fall, Tabernacles in the fall, Passover in the spring, and Pentecost in the early summer. Passover in a sense becomes the Christian Easter—the New Testament*

does not use the word Easter; Pentecost abides in Christianity, but as the anniversary of a particular Christian occasion mentioned in Acts 2. Passover and Pentecost, though retained, become radically altered, Passover to the point of a lack of recognition; all the other events in the Jewish calendar disappear from Christian usage and practice.[11]

The Rabbi penned the above words more than five decades ago with a high degree of accuracy. Hopefully, the teaching of Bible prophecy scholars and others over the intervening years has made some progress. Especially in the area of Replacement Theology, in which much of the Church has seen Israel having no place in End Times theology with her place having been taken over by the Church as the real Israel, do we hope for far better study and interpretation. Again, we need to reiterate that while we are not in any sense advocating a return to practicing the Jewish calendar and the solemn assemblies God calls for there, we must be aware of the value of seeing the activity of Jesus the Messiah in light of the truths of God's commands to the Jewish people.

The writer of Hebrews has a statement which has often caused me to wonder just what he had in mind. Maybe the Millenial period under the reign of Messiah is the answer. In concluding his great chapter of the roll call of Old Testament saints, the author says this: "These were all commended for their faith, yet none of them received what had been promised. God had planned something better for us so that only together with us would they be made perfect" (Hebrews 11:39f).

While there is much we don't yet understand about the relationship of Christian to Jewish believers, it is obvious that God has a great plan for all people and in the end we will discover it is

118

the same plan. We will greatly enrich our own faith as Christians as we seek to discover our Jewish roots and how God's ultimate purpose will be seen drawing these two families of faith together until, under the Lordship of Messiah Jesus, we will discover that we are being perfected together.

Chapter Notes

1. Zola Levitt, *The Seven Feasts of Israel*, Zola Levitt Ministries, Inc., Dallas TX, ©1979, p. 1.
2. Ibid., p. 2.
3. Scott McAllister, seventheory.com, downloaded Feb. 10, 2014, p. 2.
4. John J. Parsons, *Hebrew for Christians*, downloaded Feb. 10, 2014, p.2.
5. Levitt, op. cit., p. 9.
6. Alfred J. Kolatch, *The Jewish Book of WHY*, Jonathan David Publishers, Inc., Middle Village, NY, ©1981, p.249
7. Victor Buksbazen, *The Feasts of Israel*, Christian Literature Crusade, W. Collingwood, NJ, © 1954, p.27f
8. Ibid, p. 42.
9. Levitt, op. cit., p. 16.
10. Kolatch, op. cit., p. 247.
11. Samuel Sandmel, *A Jewish Understanding of the New Testament*, Skylight Paths Publishing, Woodstock, VT, © 2005, p. 75f.

Study Five

The Plan for Israel in The New Testament

The Apostle Paul sees Israel and the Church

If you wanted to find an authority on what God has in mind for Israel and the Hebrew people in the End-Times, to whom could you turn? In spite of all the Old Testament learning of both scholars and ordinary Jewish people, most do not seem to have a clear understanding of how their own history is going to conclude. On the other hand, most Christians, even with a rather exhaustive knowledge of the Old Testament, are unable to enunciate the relationship between these two great peoples who both serve the same God.

Surely there must be someone who can bridge the divide and help us understand and come to clarity of mind about how these people relate to the Lord and to each other as we rapidly approach dramatic events at the end of this age. Where can we find such a person?

The answer is really quite apparent if we think on it for a moment. Who has been both a Jew of the Jews and the great Apostle of the Christians? When we say it that way, the answer is obvious! It has to be the Jewish fanatic Saul who was intent on destroying the Christian faith wherever he found it. And it was also Paul who, after a face to face encounter with Jesus on the road to Damascus, became the Apostolic leader of the Christian movement.

This one person, Saul who became Paul, not only was the evangelistic individual who led the way in taking the Gospel to as much of the world as he could possibly cover, he was also the writer of a great portion of the New Testament. In those writings, he brought together his Jewish background and his new-found faith in Jesus which gives us great insight into the question of how Jews and Christians should see their relationship. This is especially crucial as we face the prophetic scenarios that await us in future days.

The Apostle's own words give us confidence in looking to him for understanding of God's plan for Israel in the future. He gives us an abbreviated *curriculum vitae* in writing to the Philippians.

If anyone else thinks he has reasons to put confidence in the flesh, I have more: circumcised on the eighth day, of the people of Israel, of the tribe of Benjamin, a Hebrew of Hebrews; in regard to the law, a Pharisee; as for zeal, persecuting the church; as for legalistic righteousness, faultless. But whatever was to my profit I now consider loss for the sake of Christ. What is more, I consider everything a loss compared to the surpassing greatness of knowing Christ Jesus my Lord, for whose sake I have lost all things (Philippians 3:4-8).

When we put this testimony along side his zeal and methodology in reaching people for Jesus as he himself states it, we can certainly find ample reason to look to Paul for assistance in knowing what God says is in store for the Jews.

Though I am free and belong to no man, I make myself a slave to everyone, to win as many as possible. To the Jews I became like a Jew, to win the Jews. To those under the law I became like one under the law (though I myself am not under the law), so as to win those under the law. To those not having the law I became like one not having the law (though I am not free from God's law but am under Christ's law), so as to win those not having the law. To the weak I became weak, to win the weak. I have become all things to all men so that by all possible means I might save some (1 Corinthians 9:19-22).

With this confidence in hand, let us in this study look to Paul's letter to the Roman Christians as he explains to them both God's plan for Israel in the end times and the intimate relationship which exists between the two. Here we find information that is clear, concise and comprehensive.

The Desire for Israel's Salvation

We do not have the space here to print all the applicable Scripture, so please read the suggested portion to give you the needed background for these discussions. For this section, please read Romans 10:1-4.

While Paul has found Jesus as his Messiah, he carries a deep burden for his people, the Jews. We know that God gave him a heart for the salvation of all men, but especially the Jews. Nowhere is this expressed more passionately than in verse one: "Brothers, my heart's desire and prayer to God for the Israelites is that they may be saved" (Romans 10:1). It is a short sentence, but it enunciates the heartbeat of the Apostle. Even though God was opening doors for him to spread the Gospel message to non-Jews, he longed to see his own people receiving Christ as well.

What does this tell us about God's plan? Since Paul's letter to the Romans is universally recognized as sacred Scripture and that we are told in the Scriptures that they were written by men as they were moved by the Spirit, we must conclude that this passage including Paul's prayer is Spirit directed as well. Thus, it seems that we can safely conclude that since Paul was praying and writing in the Spirit, this statement also reflects God's desire for the people of Israel.

Read Romans 9:2-5. Paul just a chapter earlier as we read here gives us a personal glimpse into the intensity of his longing to see the Hebrew people come to Christ. He tells us, "For I could wish that I myself were cursed and cut off from Christ for the sake of my brothers, those of my own race, the people of Israel" (vs. 3). We often claim that we are really concerned for the salvation of our loved ones and, indeed, all persons. But how ready are we to say that our burden for them is so great that we would be willing to be cut off from our Savior Jesus if it would bring others to Him? It is interesting in this same passage from chapter 9 that Paul gives us a brief resumé of just who these Israelites are. Think about the implications of these words:

> *Theirs is the adoption as sons, theirs the divine glory, the covenants, the receiving of the law, the temple worship and the promises. Theirs are the patriarchs, and from them is traced the human ancestry of Christ, who is God over all, forever praised! Amen* (vss. 4-7).

When we reflect upon these words we cannot but realize the tremendous debt which we as Christians owe the Jewish people. This certainly should move us toward an examination of our spiritual roots and what is the appropriate present-day connection to these people.

These words of the Apostle give us a preview of the direction in which God is moving in our day. We are privileged to be living in the time when we can see history racing toward the day for which Paul prays, the day the people of Israel will come to salvation.

Old Testament Prophets Quoted

Like other New Testament writers, Paul looks to the Old Testament prophets as he writes. He lays a foundation for his teaching that is firmly rooted in the Scriptures that were already familiar. This is a key concept we need to continually remind ourselves to apply. If we would fully understand the New

Testament Scriptures, we must study them in the context of their Old Testament roots. When we forget to do so, we will undoubtedly arrive at either false or incomplete conclusions.

For instance, Paul states in Romans 11:26 that, "All Israel will be saved." That has caused many people to be confused thinking that the Apostle is referring to all Jews of all time. If they would read that statement in the context of Paul's entire epistle, they would discover that that is precisely what Paul is not saying.

So that his readers would know precisely who would be saved, he quotes a major Old Testament prophet:

> "Isaiah cries out concerning Israel: 'Though the number of the Israelites be like the sand by the sea, **only the remnant will be saved**. For the Lord will carry out his sentence on earth with speed and finality'" (Romans 9:27 emphasis added).

There it is straight and simple, it is a surviving remnant who will be saved. If we would go back to Isaiah 10:20-23, from which Paul quotes, we would discover that Isaiah not only said it once but four times in those four verses; it is a surviving remnant.

My father, in scolding me, would often say after giving me a warning for the second or third time, "I don't want to have to tell you again." In other words, I was to believe and to remember what he said. The same is true for God. When He has one of his prophets tell us four times in a row that the surviving remnant of Israel will be saved, He ought not to have to keep repeating it for us. But, because many of us who are believers in Yeshua think only as New Testament Christians, we fail to seek to understand our Scriptures in light of the First Covenant.

Paul continues in Romans 9:28, by quoting the next verse from Isaiah's prophecy. Those rather disheartening words are, "The Lord, the Lord Almighty, will carry out the destruction decreed upon the whole land" (Isaiah 10:24). If we haven't done at least some basic prophecy study, the reason for this quote may not be evident. However, if we have made at least a little effort in that direction, we will probably quite quickly pick up on the fact that this verse is a reference to the Tribulation period. Paul is indicating that the salvation of the Jews is closely related to the Tribulation.

When Jesus returns at the end of the Tribulation and quickly puts an end to the rebellion of the world's armies in what we usually term the battle or campaign of Armageddon, the Jews will recognize Him as the Messiah whom they have not previously recognized. A few days later, most likely during the annual observance of the Day of Atonement, they will come to Messiah in repentance. God's wrath during the Tribulation is going to be a horrible time. Yet, God has a loving purpose in it. He will use it to bring the Jews unto Himself.

So in these three brief verses Paul gives us a great deal of enlightenment. He tells us that only the surviving remnant of the Jews will come to salvation, and that event will take place after the seven year period of world-wide destruction prepares the Jews for that long-awaited step of faith. Yes, Paul firmly roots his teaching in the Old Testament Scriptures.

Teaching by Rhetorical Questions

The Apostle Paul is a master teacher. He utilizes a wide variety of approaches in his lessons. One method in which he seems to delight and which is quite effective is the use of rhetorical questions. One purpose of the rhetorical question is to grab attention. Often the answer to the question is obvious and an answer is not expected from the hearers. Another use is to build on the obvious answer to make a further comment and maybe a not as readily agreed upon point.

At any rate, Paul used this technique with great effectiveness. This is especially true in chapters ten and eleven of Romans where he asks a series of these questions, some of them in quite rapid succession. A quick survey of these questions and the answers that Paul himself gives enlighten to us on some important issues about the Jewish people and their role in the future.

In the first portion of Romans 10, Paul sets forth a concise description of salvation and how it is available to all through faith in Jesus Christ. These key verses read, "As the Scripture says, 'Anyone who trusts in him will never be put to shame.' For there is no difference between Jew and Gentile—the same Lord is Lord of all and richly blesses all who call on him, for, 'Everyone who calls on the name of the Lord will be saved'" (Romans 10:11-13). The important point to grasp here is that the way of salvation is the same for both Jews and Gentiles; it is through faith in the Lord Jesus.

Stuart Briscoe has commented at this point, "Having established the universal relevance of the Christian gospel, Paul engages in some relentlessly logical rhetorical questioning."[1] Paul quickly heaps four of these questions one on top of another. He asks,

> "How, then, can they call on the one they have not believed in? And how can they believe in the one of whom

they have not heard? And how can they hear without someone preaching to them? And how can they preach unless they are sent?" (Romans 10:14f).

These questions often form the basis for sermons on witnessing and evangelism for Christian congregations. And that seems like a good and plausible secondary application of Paul's questions. The context, however, should not be missed. He is addressing the issue of why more Jewish persons are not coming to Messiah in faith. While the truth is, as we have already suggested, the totality of the Jewish remnant who are alive at the coming of Yeshua in power and great glory at the end of the Tribulation will come to faith in Messiah. However, it is not God's intent that any be lost and His desire is for as many Hebrews as will to come to faith during this time of the Church age. His salvation is not postponed until some later time; it is offered to all, including the Jews, at the present moment.

So the implicit answer to Paul's four-in-one rhetorical question is that they are not receiving Messiah by faith because believing Christians are not being aggressive in sharing the Gospel message with them. This certainly has profound implications for end-times ministries. Evangelism to the Jews should not be left to a few Messianic Jewish organizations. This should be a strategic part of every local congregation's evangelistic efforts, where there are Jewish persons in the community, because it is high on God's priority list. Briscoe pulls no punches in addressing this issue:

> *The key to the relative failure of the church appears to be in the "sending" of those who can reach the unreached. There is no possibility that the principles of speaking,*

hearing, believing, calling, and saving do not work because the Lord, Himself, has promised that they will function in blessing. The only possible flaw in the system must lie in the sending, and it would appear that perhaps the church has failed to understand in some measure the link between "confession with the mouth" and being sent as a herald so that people can hear, believe, call, and be saved.[2]

From this point, Paul moves to asking questions one at a time. The first of these is, "Did they not hear?" In quick reply he answers, "Of course they did" (Romans 10:18) and goes on to quote from Psalm 19:4 that the message has gone forth to the ends of the world. He immediately follows this with a logical follow-up question, "Did Israel not understand?" (Romans 10:19).

He goes on to quote from Moses and Isaiah indicating that God is using people who are not a nation like Israel to make the Jews envious. The idea is that if these unenlightened Gentiles can understand, surely you Jews should be able to as well. Paul concludes this set of questions by quoting God from Isaiah 65:2, "All day long I have held out my hands to a disobedient and obstinate people."

With that background, the once zealot persecutor of Christians, moves to four more pertinent rhetorical questions. These all are extremely important for the Church and its ministry as they seek to truly know what God's design for the future of the Jews is as we function in a world that is largely anti-Semitic. In other words, how can Christians love the Jews and desire salvation for them in a world that largely hates them and, in great measure, is working toward their demise as a people?

Paul then asks in light of the previous questions, "Did God reject his people?" (Romans 11:1). Since they are described by God as disobedient and obstinate, we might tend toward thinking that is what God would do. But Paul's answer to his own question is powerful and direct, "By no means! . . .God did not reject his people whom he foreknew" (vs. 2). These two verses alone are cause to not believe in that which much of Christianity has believed for hundreds of years, that God has rejected His people Israel and replaced them with the Church as the true Israel. Make no mistake in your thinking, God's design for Israel is alive and well!

After clarifying the issue of God's rejection of the Jews, Paul writes of Elijah and the prophet's attitude that Israel had all turned against God and that he alone was left as a faithful servant and they were attempting to kill him—a real pity party. It is appropriate here to raise the name of Elijah for the people would be aware that he will play a major role in the end times. Elijah's role was always to call the nation of Israel to repentance. In Malachi 4:5 God says, "See, I will send you the prophet Elijah before that great and terrible day of the Lord comes." In other words, it is to be expected that the prophet will come to once again call Israel to repentance just before the return of Messiah in power and great glory at the end of the Tribulation.

Thus comes another of the Apostle's questions: "And what was the Lord's answer to him?" Without time for anyone to attempt an answer, we hear the quote from God, "I have reserved for myself seven thousand who have not bowed the knee to Baal" (Romans 11:4). That was the remnant in Elijah's day. A truth we must not neglect is that God always has His remnant of faithful persons, whether we are speaking of Christians or Jews. Paul indicates that this was true of the Jews in his day as well, "So too, at the present time there is a remnant chosen by grace" (Romans 11:5).

We learn from Paul's use of rhetorical questions that the answer to one questions tends to inevitably lead to another query. So we find him, as soon as the answer is given that there is a remnant who will be saved, asking about those who are not a part of the remnant, "What then?" Once again, he is prepared with the answer and says, "What Israel sought so earnestly it did not obtain, but the elect did. The others were hardened, but as it is written: 'God gave them a spirit of stupor, eyes so that they could not see and ears so that they could not hear, to this very day'" (Romans 11:7f). So God has not rejected them, but only hardens their hearts as they refuse to see and hear.

Today we see this hardness being lived out in Judaism. While there are many Jews turning to Messiah, the vast majority are not. Most of the Jewish nation today are what we would call secular Jews, but there is a large number who are religious observant Jews. They go through the ritual, but their hearts are still hardened towards God and His Messiah. So salvation is available to all who will accept, but national Israel is suffering from hardness of heart until Messiah comes.

Again, the answer to the Apostle's previous question leads to a final one that is all important. "Again I ask: Did they stumble so as to fall beyond recovery?" God wants us to be so certain of His end times plan for the Jews that He has Paul spell it out for us in several different forms. He does not want us to miss it. Hear Paul's power answer to his own question of whether the Jews are beyond grace and beyond help and hope. "Not at all! Rather, because of their transgression, salvation has come to the Gentiles to make Israel envious" (Romans 11:11).

So, it is obvious that God wants Christian believers to realize that He still has a plan moving forward for Israel. As we contemplate what the end times mean for us, we can only comprehend the fullness of what we study as we reckon with the Jews. The world today is attempting to deal with Abraham's seed by getting rid of those whom God calls His chosen ones.

As believers we need to realize that God has designed His working with all persons in a special way. Paul enunciates this quite clearly for us, "I am not ashamed of the gospel, because it is the power of God for the salvation of everyone who believes: first for the Jew, then for the Gentile" (Romans 1:16). I am delighted that God has provided through His Son the Lord Jesus for my salvation. I have no problem with recognizing that salvation came to others, including the Jews, before me.

The Two Olive Trees

Having laid a solid foundation of God's continuing love for and plan for the nation of Israel, Paul next moves on to teach about the relationship between Christian believers and Judaism. He uses a symbol that would have been very familiar to all of Israel and to the early Christians who were coming from their Jewish background. The Olive tree is one of the symbols of Israel, two others being the fig tree and the vine. When we recognize these Jewish backgrounds, it is possible to have a much more accurate interpretation of the Christian Scriptures.

Paul introduces the concept of the olive tree in Romans 11:16 by referring to the root and the branches, ". . .if the root is holy, so are the branches." The root would refer to the patriarchs, Abraham,

133

Isaac and Jacob, and the branches to the Jewish people. This opens the door for Paul to then illustrate the relationship of Israel, the natural olive tree, and the Gentiles whom he calls the wild olive branches. We find several essential truths concerning this relationship in Romans 11:17-24. These are some of the most important verses in the Bible for Christian believers who are anxious to know more of their spiritual roots.

In verse 17, Paul says, "If some of the branches have been broken off" and refers to hardened Israel. Individual Israelites are the branches on the cultivated or natural olive tree. But, many have been broken off because of the hardness of their hearts, We remember back in 11:7 that those Jews who did not receive the grace they were looking for were hardened, or made unable to respond to the salvation that was offered by God.

In contrast, Paul says in the same verse, ". . .and you, though a wild olive shoot, have been grafted in among the others." Here he is addressing Gentile believers and explaining to them that they are, by faith in Yeshua, a part of Israel. This is key for understanding who we are in relationship to Israel and to the covenants and promises of God as well. We do not become Jews, but we become an integral part of God's larger family of faith when we become disciples of Jesus, whom we most often fail to recognize as the Messiah. In that sense, we are very much like the Jews; we miss what ought to be obvious to us.

Paul keeps building on his metaphor of the olive tree and indicates how Christians are dependent upon Israel for spiritual growth and nourishment. Those grafted in "now share in the nourishing sap from the olive root" and "consider this: You do not support the root, but the root supports you" (vs. 17f).

We fail to study our Jewish roots and thus find ourselves lacking in nourishment which we should be drawing from the olive tree. Far too often, we have distanced ourselves from our Hebrew roots and have brought spiritual deprivation upon ourselves. We have failed to realize how dependent we are upon the roots which we find described in the Old Testament. In addition, Paul indicates that Christians are prone to be boastful considering themselves, because of their faith in receiving the Messiah, greater than the Jewish branches. He strongly says, "Do not boast over those branches" (vs. 18).

Paul continues his study of the olive branches by warning Christians about their attitude which may lead them to say that "Branches were broken off so that I could be grafted in" (vs. 19). His warning is strong: "But they were broken off because of unbelief, and you stand by faith. Do not be arrogant, but be afraid. For if God did not spare the natural branches, He will not spare you either" (vs. 20f). Apparently Paul saw a spirit of arrogance among some of the Christians and he reminded them that they were in danger of being cut off as well if they fell into unbelief.

Rabbi Sandmel has written of this passage with a clear Jewish perspective and says,

> *Gentiles are not to vaunt themselves over Jews, however, because Gentiles are only branches grafted onto the tree of Judaism. After the period of the hardening of the hearts of the Jews has passed, God will revert to Israel and save them. Israel's blindness was an opportunity for the eyes of Gentiles to be opened.*[3]

William Greathouse has likewise commented on this verse, but from a Wesleyan/Arminian perpective:

> The continuity between Israel and Gentile believers is not intrinsic; it rests solely on God's faithfulness and their continuing faith. God did not spare Israel when she fell into unbelief; neither will He preserve Gentile Christians unless they stand fast by **faith** and **continue in his goodness** (22; cf. 8:17; Col. 1:21-23).[4]

Paul then moves to sound a clarion call that while God is stern, He is still a gracious God who is willing to accept anyone who will repent and turn their back on unbelief. The Apostle says of the Jews, "And if they do not persist in unbelief, they will be grafted in, for God is able to graft them in again" (vs. 23). In other words, the Jews were not cut off from God's grace eternally by their rejection of Jesus as the Messiah; He is waiting for them to return in faith and belief and be restored to Himself.

The zealous Jew turned zealous Christian completes his discourse on the relationship of the wild and natural olive trees with a bit of a naturalist's analysis. He says, "After all, if you were cut out of an olive tree that is wild by nature, and contrary to nature were grafted into a cultivated olive tree, how much more readily will these, the natural branches, be grafted into their own olive tree!" (vs. 24).

As a final argument in the olive tree discussion, Paul indicates that he knows that there is a flaw in his argument that those acquainted with the process of grafting will immediately pick up on. He says that the process of grafting wild branches onto a cultivated tree is "contrary to nature."

What does he mean? Greathouse clarifies this grafting procedure which may be something most of us know little about:

> *It is a process never performed in horticulture. The cultivated branch is always engrafted upon the wild stock, and never the other way around. Paul disarms his critics by acknowledging that he is aware of the unnaturalness of the particular kind of grafting he describes. But if, **contrary to nature**, God has grafted wild olive branches into His cultivated tree, certainly He is able to graft the natural branches in again. The restoration of Israel is a divine possibility.*[5]

At the time of Israel's coming to faith in *Yeshua ha Mashiach*, it will be entirely in keeping with God's character to receive them and restore them to the olive tree that has been theirs all along, but because of their hardness of heart they were as branches broken off. The corollary is true as well. The people of Israel will feel so natural in coming to Messiah Jesus in faith that it will be a wondrous day of rejoicing for them as they experience the love of the eternal Father who has called them to be His own people, to walk with Him, to experience His blessings and to be a blessing to all the nations of the world.

Prophecy teacher Bill Cloud expands on this thought and notes the unity between the natural and wild olive branches.

> *Please notice that the branch Paul describes as being grafted into the cultivated olive tree is also an olive branch, albeit a wild one (Rom. 11:24). Nevertheless, it is not a fig branch or a myrtle branch. It is an olive branch, which means it originated from the same species of seed as did the cultivated tree! Why is that important? Because the Torah*

teaches that there can be no mingling of species of seed, or else the field (Lev. 19:19), the vineyard (Deut. 22:9), or in this case, the tree is defiled.

That they are of the same "seed" but are also from the nations strongly indicates that Abraham's seed is comprised of those who are of faith and not necessarily those of blood. This is a point Paul strives to make throughout his ministry in most, if not all, of his epistles.

In the end, there is only one tree, not two, in Romans 11. In Galatians 3 Paul notes that there is neither Jew nor Greek.[6]

God is the God of restoration and His will is to restore all things as they were in the beginning. Truly, the teaching of the olive branches is an undeniable example of that truth. J. Dwight Pentecost writes of the nature of Israel's conversion, noting not only its individual impact, but also that of the nation's destiny.

Since no unsaved person is to enter the millennium, Israel anticipated a conversion that would prepare them for this promised kingdom. The second advent will witness this conversion of the nation, that is, all true Israel, so the covenants given to them may find fulfillment during the age of the Messiah's reign.[7]

In the next verse, Paul gives us the reason for his extensive teaching on the relationship of the cultivated and wild olives branches. Paul has a great desire for his readers to be informed and knowledgeable about the things of faith. So he writes, "I do not want you to be ignorant of this mystery, brothers, so that you may not be conceited" (vs. 25) This is the type verse we can almost ignore, but it has several very important truths that we must grasp.

138

First Paul wisely teaches so that Christians may not lack knowledge and understanding of the deep concepts of the faith. It is very evident today, even though multitudes of Christians carry their Bible with them faithfully, they have never really grasped the nature of the relationship which exists between themselves and the Jewish people.

Secondly, the Apostle talks of "this mystery." In the New Testament, mystery does not mean something that is mysterious. Rather, the term refers to the fact that a truth that has not been generally known previously is now being revealed. So the mystery of the olives trees was being revealed by Paul to the Church in his day. We ought to very carefully study the things that the New Testament speaks of as mysteries for they are usually very key concepts that will be helpful in our walk of faith, especially as we anticipate the events of the end-times.

A third emphasis we find in verse 25 as well as in previous verses is that, as believers who are recipients of the grace of God because of the unbelief of the Israelites, we dare not become conceited or develop an attitude of superiority over those whom God called first into a walk of faith. Our relationship to Israel through faith should humble us and not make us prideful. Paul wrote with this same emphasis to the believers at Ephesus: "For it is by grace you have been saved, through faith—and this not from yourselves, it is the gift of God—not by works, so that no one can boast" (Ephesus 2:9).

Israel Turns to Yeshua the Messiah

Having enlightened us as to the mystery of the relationship of Christians and Jews through the olive tree metaphor, The Apostle Paul plunges immediately into the logical conclusion of his argument: how the Jews come to salvation. This is an exciting portion of Scripture as it relates hows God's purpose in End Times prophecy comes to a climax with the salvation of the Jews. This is, indeed, a turning point in human history as God's plan for a wonderful time of peace under the Lordship of His Son is ready to begin.

We concluded our last topic with a look at the first section of Romans 11:25. Without missing a breath, Paul begins with the final portion of the verse to give us details of the coming to faith of the surviving remnant of Israel. Of particular concern to Paul are the matters of the timing when the fullness of the Gentiles is complete and the nature of the hardening which has come temporarily to the Hebrews.

"Israel has experienced a hardening in part until the full number of the Gentiles has come in. And so all Israel will be saved" (Romans 11:25b, 26a). This is the heart of the issue which Paul is discussing. The majestic question is, will the Hebrew people ever come to faith as a people or simply a few as individual persons? Paul's use of the phrase "all Israel" makes it abundantly clear that there is a day approaching when the Jewish people will come *en masse* to know Christ Jesus as Messiah and Savior.

As we have already said, this does not mean all Jews of all time. Rather it refers to the remnant of the Jews who survive the Tribulation and are alive at the time of the return of Jesus. But how does their salvation occur? Paul makes it quite clear that they will come like every other believer, by coming to Jesus in faith, repenting of their sin and receiving God's forgiveness. At that moment they will not only become followers of Messiah Jesus, they will be grafted back into the natural olive tree as Paul explained in the preceding verses.

It is also very unmistakable to whom they come for salvation. The Apostle quotes Isaiah 59:30, 31 which is a most familiar Scripture: "The deliverer will come from Zion, he will turn godlessness away from Judah. And this is my covenant with them when I take away their sins" (Romans 11:26b, 27). The deliverer who is coming to the Jews from Mount Zion is the Lord Jesus who will be the One to provide the means of salvation. Then God says that He Himself will be making a new covenant with them as they receive their forgiveness. It is the covenant of having His law written on their hearts rather than on tablets of stone. God makes this promise at many places and this is the time it will come to fruition.

A key touch-point in the Jewish/Christian relationship is at this very point. The Jews will come to Jesus in the same manner as every Christian believer. They will recognize Jesus as the Messiah, they will confess their sins, call on His name and be saved. There is no reason to be concerned that somehow the Jews are going to be saved on the basis of their works or animal sacrifices. Everyone comes to God the same way: through faith in Jesus Christ.

Just prior to making his almost unbelievable statement of Israel's salvation, Paul expresses an explanatory concept regarding why Israel has not as a nation come to salvation prior to the time in the future of which he speaks. He indicates that "Israel has

141

experienced a hardening in part until the full number of the Gentiles has come in" (Romans 11:25b). To understand this phrase we must regard it in the context of the next few verses which are packed with powerful theological significance. Let's consider some of these ideas in a very brief way. There are six aspects of Israel's hardening which we can easily note.

The first truth to be noted is that Israel's hardening is only in part; it is not total and it is not eternal. We understand this from the plain statement in verse 25 that it is a hardening "in part." That is the reason that we have seen Jewish persons coming to faith in Messiah over the years. In recent times since the coming to statehood, many Jewish people are receiving Jesus as their Savior. It is reported that there are now more than 150 messianic Jewish congregations in Israel. So not all hearts are hardened to the Gospel.

Neither is it a hardening that continues forever. The Apostle indicates a time of ending of this hardness when the fullness of the Gentiles has come in. That will apparently take place at the time of the Rapture of the Bride when the ministry of the primarily Gentile Church will be complete.

That leads us to conclude that secondly Israel's hardness is only temporary. How can we best understand what the term "full number of the Gentiles" refers to? This can be a bit tricky as we can easily confuse this statement with those regarding the ending of the times when the Gentiles have concluded overrunning Jerusalem, often referred to as the "times of the Gentiles." That event will not conclude until the end of the Tribulation when Messiah returns. So, it is apparent that Paul is here referring to the Church.

It is doubtful that the "full number of Gentiles" refers to a specific numerical count of those Gentiles who have become believers.

God in his infinite knowledge knows exactly what that number will be, but it is doubtful that He is standing on the sidelines awaiting the count to come in. Much more likely, it is a reference to the time of completeness of the ministry of the Church to which Paul refers. Matthew Henry is helpful at this point and defines the moment as,

> . . .*when the gospel has had its intended success, and made its progress in the Gentile world. The Jews shall continue in blindness, until God has performed his whole work among the Gentiles. God's taking them [Jews] again was not because he had need of them, but of his own free grace.*[8] (clarification added)

The third aspect of Israel's hardness is how it will be turned aside. A quote from Isaiah 59:20 indicates that "The deliverer [Redeemer in Isaiah] will come from Zion; he will turn away godlessness from Jacob" (Romans 11:26f). This is more than deliverance from the enemies of Israel; it is deliverance or redemption from their sinfulness. Thus, it is a rather pointed reference to the fact that when Messiah comes, there will be a spiritual turning to Him. We understand this point to be so from the prophecy given through Zechariah 12:10, "They will see him whom they have pierced."

The fourth truth we find is that at the time of Israel's salvation, they are given a new covenant by the Lord. Israel is a people who have been bound to the Lord by His covenants with them beginning with Abraham. So, when they come to receive Messiah, it is not surprising that they become partakers of a new covenant in Christ Jesus, "And this is my covenant with them when I take away their sin" (Romans 11:27).

The covenant God is referring to is most certainly the one which God spoke through Jeremiah:

> *"This is the covenant I will make with the house of Israel after that time," declares the Lord. "I will put my law in their minds and write it on their hearts. I will be their God, and they will be my people. . . .For I will forgive their wickedness and will remember their sins no more"* (Jeremiah 31:33, 34b).

This is a most significant detail to capture when we are reflecting upon the relationship between Christian believers and Messianic believers; both are a part of the New Covenant in Christ Jesus. God is always consistent. The New Covenant which Jesus spoke of as being in His blood is for all who will trust in Him. Paul clarified this earlier in his letter.

> *As the Scripture says, "Anyone who trusts in him will never be put to shame." For there is no difference between Jew and Gentile—the same Lord is Lord of all and richly blesses all who call on him, for, "Everyone who calls on the name of the Lord will be saved"* (Romans 10:11-13).

God began his relationship with the Hebrews by calling Abraham and establishing covenant with him and other covenants with his descendents. Thus, the final conclusion will be that they will be a part of the New Covenant in Christ Jesus. As Gentiles, we are not bound by the former covenants, but are the beneficiaries of them. And, with the Jews we are bound together in the New Covenant of faith when they turn to the Lord as have ourselves and others before them.

Many are quite willing to assign Jews to a place of eternal damnation because of their rejection of Jesus when He came in His first Advent. To so believe is to deny a basic tenet of God's character. He does not go back on His word. Paul spells this out with utter clarity: ". . .but as far as election is concerned, they are loved on account of the patriarchs, for God's gifts and his call are irrevocable" (Romans 11:28b, 2). In other words, God does not reject the Jews because they rejected the Messiah. It is against His very nature to go back on His word.

When God makes a promise, it is forever. While man is free to accept or reject the proffered gift, the offer is not withdrawn. Israel's hardening will be overruled by God's election of His people.

Finally, Paul deals with a very difficult aspect of Israel's hardened hearts. In essence, he says that all men are disobedient, and thus in need of His mercy.

Just as you who were at one time disobedient to God have now received mercy as a result of their disobedience, so they too have now become disobedient in order that they too may now receive mercy as a result of God's mercy to you. For God has bound all men over to disobedience so that he may have mercy on them all (Romans 11:30-32).

The truth here may be expressed in this way: Israel's hardening because of their unbelief has made it possible for Gentiles to receive God's mercy as they turn to Messiah in faith, not by keeping the law. There is this strain of thought running through Paul's writing that our faith is able to arouse Israel to jealousy, and they will overcome their unbelief and disobedience and desperately run to Christ and receive God's mercy by faith and not by relying on the

145

works of the law. Briscoe's explanation may make it plainer than mine:

> *In his divine wisdom, God chose to use the rejection of Christ by His people as a means of reaching the Gentiles, so that through His abundant demonstration of grace to them Israel might be brought to a realization of the grace of God in Christ. The tragedy of Israel's unbelief is therefore used by God to bring about the victory of Gentile evangelization, which, in turn, will lead to Jewish restoration. . . .He has shown that even in the midst of human obduracy and rebellion, He can and will use all things to bring about His eternal purposes.*[9]

Romans chapter eleven is a marvelous portion of Scripture where we are enabled to see the end, even as God has seen it from the beginning. He has every intention of seeing His Chosen People come to faith. And we have His eternal word, revealed through Paul the Apostle, that it is going to come to pass.

How Israel is Saved

We find that Paul gives us quite a definitive statement that in spite of rejecting Jesus as the Messiah when He came in His first advent, and having suffered a hardening of heart through these intervening centuries, the Jews will ultimately come to salvation at the Second Coming. We have that issue stated as a certain fact by the Apostle. What we don't find in the Romans epistle is how that is going to take place. For that we turn to other Scriptures. While that is a study in and of itself, we will conclude this chapter with a look at three verses that will give us a capsule summary of what will happen at the time of Israel's national salvation.

The first thing that is important to note is that those Jews who survive the Tribulation period will be gathered by Jesus to Jerusalem and the surrounding area. We find this often overlooked truth enunciated by Jesus Himself in the Olivet Discourse when He was answering the disciples' questions concerning His return. He spoke of this gathering of the Jews whom He called "the elect" in this statement:

> *At that time the sign of the Son of Man will appear in the sky and all the nations of the earth will mourn. They will see the Son of Man coming on the clouds of the sky, with power and great glory. And he will send his angels with a loud trumpet call, and they will gather his elect from the four winds, from one end of the heavens to the other* (Matthew 24:30f).

This gathering, in all likelihood, will begin on the celebration of the Feast of Trumpets and continue for ten days until the Day of Atonement when Israel will come to Jesus in repentance and salvation. A great regathering to the land of Israel will be the prelude to their restoration as the people of God by faith.

Following their regathering, we read from the Old Testament prophet of their cleansing by Jesus. Listen to these very specific words of how Yeshua will meet their spiritual need. "On that day a fountain will be opened to the house of David and the inhabitants of Jerusalem, to cleanse them from sin and impurity" (Zechariah 13:1). Of course, the fountain to which God refers is the "fountain filled with blood drawn from Immanuel's vein."

The great and final unifying factor between the two parts of the Bible is nothing other than salvation in Jesus Christ, *Yeshua ha Meshiach*. The Savior of the New Testament will be recognized as the Messiah of the Old Testament. At long last, the beautiful promise of Paul which he revealed to the Galatian church will be a reality. Oh, what wonderful words! All believers in Yeshua as Messiah are the seed of Abraham!

> *You are all sons of God through faith in Christ Jesus, for all of you who were baptized into Christ have clothed yourselves with Christ. There is neither Jew nor Greek, slave nor free, male nor female, for you are all one in Christ Jesus. If you belong to Christ, then you are Abraham's seed, and heirs according to the promise* (Galatians 3:26-29).

A third critical aspect of Israel's salvation is that they call on the name of Jesus. God spoke through Zechariah and declared what would happen: "They will call on my name, and I will answer them. I will say, 'They are my people,' and they will say, 'The Lord is our God'" (Zechariah 13:9). The bottom line for those who would come to faith in God through Jesus must come in faith and ask for forgiveness and cleansing. God Himself declared this to be the pattern,

> *And it shall come to pass that whosoever shall call on the name of the Lord shall be delivered: for in mount Zion and in Jerusalem shall be deliverance, as the Lord hath said, and in the remnant whom the Lord shall call* (Joel 2:32).

We note that special mention as to whom this applies is included in the verse, "the remnant whom the Lord shall call." This verse has universal application, as attested by the fact that both Peter in preaching on the Day of Pentecost and Paul when writing to the Romans quote this verse. In other words, everyone who calls on the name of the Lord shall be saved including the surviving remnant of Israel.

The time frame for this is also specified in the preceding two verses. There it tells of the signs and wonders in heaven and on earth before the great and terrible day of the Lord comes. That puts the salvation of all the Jewish remnant at the time of the return of Jesus.

Thus, we see that Israel's salvation is consistent with that of all persons. They are called or gathered for salvation, come to Jesus for cleansing and call upon the name of Jesus. God is so consistently wonderful in the application of His grace. He plays no favorites, He has no short-cuts. But everyone who will may come to Him and be saved.

As we take the long look at the history of the Hebrews, we see that the call which went out to Abraham to be the father of a group of persons who would have a unique relationship to God Himself will finally come to fruition on the day of the Glorious Appearing of *Yeshua ha Mashiach*, Jesus the Messiah.

Chapter Notes

1. D. Stuart Briscoe, *The Communicator's Commentary*, vol. 6, Romans, Word Books, Waco, TX, © 1982, p. 200.
2. Ibid., p. 201.
3. Samuel Sandmel, *A Jewish, Understanding of the New Testament*, Skylight Paths Publishing, Woodstock, VT, © 2005, p. 94.
4. William Greathouse, *Beacon Bible Commentary*, vol. VIII, Beacon Hill Press, Kansas City, MO, © 1968, p. 226.

5. Ibid., p. 227.
6. Bill Cloud, *Enmity Between the Seeds*, Shoreshim Ministries, Cleveland, TN, © 2004, p. 101.
7. J. Dwight Pentecost, *Things to Come*, Zondervan Publishing House, Grand Rapids, MI, © 1958, p. 507.
8. *The NIV Matthew Henry Commentary*, Zondervan Publishing House, Grand Rapids, MI, © 1992, p. 593.
9. Briscoe, op. cit., p. 212.

Study Six

Israel's Conversion and Cleansing[1]

Read Zechariah 13:1-9

A Special Verse

Many years ago I was reading through the book of Zechariah and not understanding much of it at all. I had come to claim as an important verse for my life Zechariah 4:6. The words of God to Zerubbabel became somewhat of a life motto shortly after my experience of sanctification, "Not by might, nor by power, but by my spirit, saith the Lord of hosts" (KJV). So I had a little knowledge of Zechariah, with the emphasis on *little*. I'm not sure at what age or at what stage of my spiritual development I was in. I only know that it was a long time ago when I was reading and as I came to Chapter 13, something happened as I read the first verse. Somehow the

Spirit of God quickened to my spirit another verse, "On that day a fountain will be opened to the house of David and the inhabitants of Jerusalem, to cleanse them from sin and impurity."

At that time, I had little concept of Bible prophecy. I knew almost nothing of what the Old Testament prophets said of God's plan for Israel. I had no concept of when "that day" would take place. In these later years as I have come to the study of prophecy, I now comprehend why this verse was so firmly implanted within me by the Holy Spirit. It speaks of the pivotal point in history when God's special people, the Jews, will finally be brought to a place of faith and salvation. As I have worked on the study of this prophetic book, my mind has continually been focused on this verse. All of the message given by God to Zechariah wraps itself around these words.

I share my story at this point to encourage you. As you read Scripture, even when you feel you are not comprehending all that God has there for you, be open to the fact that God wants to give you a special message, an unique word especially suited to your spiritual life. In my case, I believe that God was saying that He was going to give me a ministry of studying and teaching His prophetic word. My regret is that I did not comprehend this until after so many years had elapsed. But, praise the Lord, God's Word still speaks to us with the sharpness of a double-edged sword.

The Fountain Opened

There may be a lot of verses in prophecy which are difficult to understand and which take a large measure of study. But the first verse of Zechariah 13 is not one of them. If you have allowed God to give you a basic measure of doctrinal understanding and a bit of comprehension of prophecy, you will know what this verse is about. But, if not, let's make sure we are clear. God says, "On that day a fountain will be opened." What fountain is it? We do not have to ponder long on that question. God has only one fountain that will "cleanse them from sin and impurity" (13:1). **[Note: In this study when a reference stands alone, it is from Zechariah.]** It is, of course, the fountain the song writers speak of:

> *There is a fountain filled with blood drawn from Emmanuel's veins;*
> *And sinners plunged beneath that flood, lose all their guilty stains* (William Cowper).

> *Lay aside the garments that are stained with sin, and be washed in the blood of the Lamb.*
> *There's a fountain flowing for the soul unclean, O, be washed in the blood of the Lamb* (Elisha A. Hoffman).

> *O, precious fountain that saves from sin, I am so glad I have entered in;*
> *There Jesus saves me and keeps me clean; Glory to His name* (Elisha A. Hoffman).

Many times we believe, that because of the Law, God has ordained a different way for the sin of the Jews to be forgiven. Because of that we have often drawn a line between us and the Jewish people. But, when we begin to understand God's plan for His people, we find that never has this dichotomy been present. From the promise in the Garden of Eden to Eve (Genesis 3:15), we have seen that Yeshua has always been in the mind and heart of God as the only way of salvation. The writer to the Hebrews in the New Testament has made it clear in that marvelous chapter on faith that this is so. After citing a multitude of examples of faith in Old Testament believers, what did He write?

> *These were all commended for their faith, yet none of them received what had been promised. God had planned something better for us so that only together with us would they be made perfect* (Hebrews 11:39f).

Those verses are the final ones in Chapter 11 and unfortunately we usually stop our reading there. But, for those two verses to make sense, we must continue reading in Chapter 12:

> *Let us fix our eyes on Jesus, the author and perfecter of our faith, who for the joy set before him endured the cross, scorning its shame and sat down at the right hand of the throne of God* (Hebrews 12:2).

There we have it in capsule form. The faith that every Old Testament saint had was awaiting the very thing we read of in Zechariah 12:10, "They will look on me, the one they have pierced." I believe that immediately after His death, Jesus went to the place in Hades called Abraham's bosom and allowed all those who had believed God to look to Him. They would have seen those fresh wounds of piercing. At His ascension, He took the spirits of those believing Jews with Him to Heaven, emptying forever that portion of Hades.

Now, we look forward to "that day," when all the Jewish remnant left on earth will be able to look up to Him. As they look in faith and cry out to Him, the fountain of cleansing that flows from Calvary will gush forth for their eternal salvation. God is One who shows no partiality. The same fountain provides cleansing for both Jew and Gentile.

Can it really be true that God has remembered His promises to Abraham and his descendents? Should we truly expect that there is a day coming when Israel will turn to the Lord Jesus as their Messiah? Many people, including that large group of Christians known as amillenialists [those who believe there is no literal one thousand year reign of Christ] say that the Church has replaced Israel in God's plan. Paul heard of this rumor and asked, "Did God reject his people?" and quickly answers, "By no means" (Romans 11:1). David Reagan, a leading prophecy teacher, says it well:

> *The Jewish people have been set aside as a result of God's discipline. But He has not forgotten them. In Isaiah 49:16 the Lord says He could never forget the Jewish people because He has them tattooed on the palms of His hands! In Jeremiah 31:35-37 the Lord asks, "When will the offspring of Israel cease to be a nation before Me?" His answer is that they will continue to be special in His eyes until the fixed order of the universe departs. . .That's the reason the Jews are being regathered from the four corners of the world right now. It is one of the greatest miracles of history.[2]*

The format of Zechariah 13 is somewhat unique. In the first verse we are told the fountain is opened. Then God deals with several other issues, including the rejection of the Shepherd when He came the first time. But, the effect of the open fountain does not appear until the final verse of the Chapter: "They will call on my name and I will answer them; I will say, 'They are my people,' and they will say, 'The Lord is our God'" (13:9). They have been His

155

people by His choosing since the call went out to Abraham, but now they are His by faith. Duane Lindsey gives a succinct summary of this truth,

> *On the day of Christ's crucifixion the fountain was opened potentially for all Israel and the whole world. At the second Advent of Christ, the fountain will be opened experientially for the Jewish nation.*[3]

A further look at this marvelous verse indicates that it is for "the house of David and the inhabitants of Jerusalem." This would indicate that this fountain was available not only to the line of David but to all the residents of the land.

It is significant that God indicates that the cleansing that will take place is for both "sin and uncleanness." Many perhaps would think this is just a redundant manner of speaking of salvation. But there is a deeper message here that, to a great degree, is being lost in our day. I believe that to be cleansed from sin refers to forgiveness and to be put into a right relationship with God. Here we have a further opportunity for Israel, that opportunity to be cleansed from the impurity of the heart.

The message of a second work of God's grace in believers is seldom heard in most of our churches. God says this is the experience that Israel needs; can Christians hope to live in preparation for the coming of the Bridegroom without the experience of heart holiness? The author addressed this issue of holiness in his book, *The Love Letters of Jesus*:

> *The imperative of holiness for the Bride cannot be made any plainer than we find from the author of the*

letter to the Hebrews: "Make very effort to live in peace with all men and to be holy; without holiness no one will see the Lord" (Hebrews 12:14). We can sing songs about the coming of Jesus, we can long to look upon His face, we can anticipate that because we have claimed salvation we shall be caught up when the Bridegroom calls. But the Bible speaks very clearly about this; Jesus is looking for a holy Bride. It cannot be much clearer; unholy believers are not going to hear or see the Bridegroom when He calls.[4]

I commend this verse (13:1) to you for commitment to memory. This will be the climax of history, just before we enter into the one thousand year reign of Messiah. At that time, the olive tree of Israel and its grafted-in wild olive branch will be one under the Kingship of the Lion of the tribe of Judah, the Messiah. How patient God has been in awaiting that day. But, without a doubt, we are fast approaching the day when we will see these things coming to pass. God goes on in this chapter to tell how He is going to cleanse the nation and the land as well as the people.

Idols and False Prophets Removed

God continues to talk of the same time frame as He says again "On that day." Immediately after telling of the spiritual restoration of the people to Himself, God indicates the next area of cleansing. The two problems we have previously noted that aroused God's ire were the keeping and worshiping of idols and of false prophets or false shepherds leading the flock astray. After the cleansing of the people, God tells how these problems are to be dealt with and the methods are distinct for each of them. There will be no place for them in the Kingdom of the Messiah.

The problem of idols God is going to take care of Himself and quite quickly. "'I will banish the names of the idols from the land, and they will be remembered no more,' declares the Lord Almighty" (13:2). This reminds me of creation; God speaks it and it is so. It recalls the plan for the conclusion of Armageddon; the word of His mouth, the double-edged sword, brings it to an end. Now He speaks a word to banish the names of the idols and they are forgotten.

It is significant that God is not concerned with getting rid of the idols themselves. They are simply objects of wood or stone with no power. The power of an idol comes when we give it a name and attach authority and power to it. This issue is so important that God gave Moses the injunction about idols as the second commandment.

On the issue of the name of idols we have a strong word from the Apostle Peter, "Salvation is found in no one else, for there is no other name under heaven given to men by which we must be saved" (Acts 4:12). It is all in the name of Jesus, "the name that is above every name" (Philippians 2:9). It is quite obvious that in matters of the spirit we tend to overlook the importance of names.

The problem of false prophets is handled differently. God simply says, "I will remove both the prophets and the spirit of impurity from the land" (13:2). He then goes on to relate how this removal will occur. The key to watch for here is that the spirit of impurity is gone. That means that the Spirit of purity can do its work. So, many of the false prophets will disappear because the impure spirit within them has departed. There will be some who will continue their vile practice and their demise will be left to their families as noted in verse three. This is a reference to how false prophets were to be handled in the Law according to Deuteronomy 18:20-22. This death penalty, while seldom enacted, was to be carried out by the next of kin (See related reference in Deuteronomy 13:6-11). Another way the false prophets will be dispensed is by shame, "On that day every prophet will be ashamed of his prophetic vision" (13:4). Because of their shame after a new spirit has come upon them, they will attempt to hide the fact that they have been posing as prophets. Some who had been wearing clothing to identify themselves as prophets will cease to do so. He will claim that he is a farmer. And the fake prophets with self-inflicted wounds of idol worshipers will be claiming that the wounds were from discipline inflicted by his friends (13:4-6).

God loves those true prophets who faithfully proclaim His message to the people; but He hates those who pretend to be His prophets but do not listen to His voice. Thus, we note two essential things God immediately removes from people of faith: idols and false prophets. A word to the wise should be sufficient. Jesus often cautions His disciples to not be deceived about these same temptations as we move toward the return of Messiah.

After a brief picture of what life will be like after Israel calls out to Messiah for salvation, God takes a backward jump. This is one of those places where we must use judicious reasoning in our reading of prophecy. We have just looked at a passage that describes the future. Now, God speaks of what was future prophecy when given to Zechariah, but which was fulfilled in the first Advent of the Messiah, so it is now history to us. But He quickly moves on once again to tell how things will be for the Jews just before Jesus returns.

Strike the Shepherd, Scatter the Sheep

In this next verse, which stands alone in a real sense, God summarizes for Zechariah's hearers what happens when the Messiah comes the first time. He does not go into detail, but uses a series of figures of speech to get His message across. He first of all speaks to an impersonal object and says, "Awake, O sword, against my shepherd" (13:7). The obvious meaning here is that the Lord Himself will direct the death of His Shepherd, the One who is the Good Shepherd in contrast to the multitude of bad and false shepherds that Israel has tolerated. That this is an obvious reference to Jesus is made clear as God continues, "against the man who is close to me." Who is closer to Him than His own dear Son? He is saying to Israel, as we remember this was future to them, that though you reject Him and He will be killed, I am the Almighty. I direct the affairs of men and of the world. Lieth has a most appropriate comment on this verse:

> The sword of God was directed against the Good Shepherd in whom was no sin. God put the guilt of man on His fellow, the Man after His own heart, who did not move from His Father's side during His life on earth, on His beloved Son in whom He had only pleasure. This verse could also be described as the heart of the Gospel. It surpasses our power of imagination, but reveals God's immeasurable love for the sinner, in that He gave the Man who was closest to Him for us.[5]

The result of the death of the Savior is given in a simple equation, "Strike the shepherd and the sheep will be scattered" (13:7). This could have several different meanings, or all of them could be true. We know that after the crucifixion, many disciples were scattered and later, because of persecution, most of Jesus' disciples were dispersed from Jerusalem. This latter idea of the persecution of the early Church could be the meaning of "and I will turn my hand against the little ones" referring to the immaturity of the early believers. The scattering of the sheep could also be applied to the Jewish nation as they were scattered following the destruction of Jerusalem in 70 A.D.

At any rate, we see a cyclic pattern of scattering and regathering which occupies a central place in prophecy. We may be certain, that though God's people may be scattered for either a short or long period, they will be regathered unto the Father at the time which He designates.

Bad News, Good News

As we approach verse eight of Zechariah Chapter 13, we find God using another technique of prophecy that we may find a bit confusing. It is what is sometimes called telescoping of prophecies. This occurs where a prophecy of one time period is telescoped into a later time period. If we fail to note the change of time frame, we may make serious errors in interpretation. In this present scenario, God has been speaking of the scattering of the sheep which will take place following the death of the Messiah at His first appearance. Then we read, "'In the whole land,' declares the Lord, 'two-thirds will be struck down and perish; yet one third will be left in it'" (13:8). To what time is God referring here?

We must assume, because of other Scriptures, that God is now referring again to a time when Israel has gathered back in the land in great numbers. The terrible wrath that will be coming on the people during the last half of the Tribulation is so severe that they will again be scattered as they flee to any place that might offer safety. So we have the common thread of scattering which will recur once again. But, not all will escape to safety. Two-thirds of the people "in the whole land" will die. This is consistent with what we read in Revelation 9:15, 18, 20.

Even though one-third will not be killed, the Lord indicates that those who remain will suffer severe testing. Here is how He describes it, "This third I will bring into the fire; I will refine them like silver and test them like gold" (13:9a).

The Revelation deals with this terrible time of wrath in much more detail. Here God just paints with a broad brush the unimaginable terror of those days, but He also with that same brush pictures the glorious conclusion for the remnant that remains. We cited the last half of verse nine earlier, but this is one of the most key statements of Zechariah's entire prophecy. We have the response to the fountain that had been available to them the entire time since Calvary. But, oh, what they have had to go through because they could not see Jesus for who He is. Finally we are enabled to hear, as Paul Harvey used to say, "the rest of the story." The covenant relationship is restored at last. It calls for bolder type:

They will call on my name and I will answer them; I will say, "They are my people," and they will say, "The Lord is our God" (13:9).

Many people today, in light of all the publicity over the Middle-east, are wondering and asking what is going to become of Israel. Here you have an answer, a word directly from God. How might things be different if our political leaders could know and understand that God has a plan for Israel that will not be thwarted. While we stand on the side-lines and wring our hands; while leaders attempt to facilitate an Israel-Palestinian two-state peace process; while we watch the nations as they ramp up their frantic attempts to annihilate the Jewish people; while we feel helpless and futile in our efforts, what can we do?

We can learn all we can about the last days. We can encourage one another with the prophetic message. We can learn to discern the signs of the times. And we can share with the world, even the world of the Church that doesn't seem interested, that God has not forgotten what He told Zechariah in Chapter 13, verse nine. He is the God who remembers Israel, and He will bring it to pass! Now would be an excellent time to claim the words of Isaiah as our own:

> *For Zion's sake I will not keep silent, for Jerusalem's sake I will not remain quiet,*
> *till her righteousness shines out like the dawn, her salvation like a blazing torch.*
> *The nations will see your righteousness, and all kings will glory;*
> *you will be called by a new name that the mouth of the Lord will bestow.*
> *You will be a crown of splendor in the Lord's hand, a royal diadem in the hand of your God* (Isaiah 62:1-3).

When we come to the final Chapter of Zechariah, we discover many exciting and awesome things that will happen following His

Glorious Appearing. The changes that will occur among people and the nations are outstanding. The marvelous renovations to the physical earth strain the imagination. The widespread holiness that will pervade the new society is fantastic.

Enduring Truths

1. Two closely related ideas, which take place at different times, as though they are parts of the same event. Sometimes in reading Bible prophecy, the Holy Spirit will quicken a specific verse or passage to minds and spirits as a future anchor point or key for understanding prophecy.
2. The fountain by which Israel will ultimately be saved is the same and only fountain of cleansing by which all persons must be saved, the blood of Jesus.
3. Those who believe in "replacement theology" say that the Church has replaced Israel in God's plan and, thus, there is no future for Israel. They are usually known as amillenialists because they do not believe in a literal 1,000 year physical reign of Messiah here on the earth.
4. The fountain opened for Israel in the last days is not a new fountain, but the one which has been waiting to flow for them when they have the faith to accept it.
5. The cleansing from impurity goes beyond the forgiveness of sin and speaks of the cleansing from the impurity of the heart.
6. The two major problems causing God's people to stray from Him are the worship of idols and the leadership of false shepherds.

7. The telescoping of prophecy occurs when God speaks of two closely related ideas, which take place at different times, as though they are parts of the same event.

8. Our present day dilemma of making sense out of the turmoil in the Middle-East must not be allowed to distract us from our commitment to believing what God has said about these times as well as Israel's future.

Chapter Notes

1. Ray Bachman, *The God Who Remembers*, Morning Star Ministries, Mountain Home, AR, © 2014, pp. 119-128 (entire chapter with editing).
2. David Reagan, *Wrath and Glory*, New Leaf Press, Green Forest, AR, © 2009, p. 127.
3. F. Duane Lindsey, *The Bible Knowledge Commentary*, Edited by John F. Walvoord and Roy B. Zuck, Victor Books, Wheaton, IL, © 1985, p. 1568.
4. Ray Bachman, *The Love Letters of Jesus*, Morning Star Ministries, Mountain Home, AR, © 2009, p. 184.
5. Norbert Lieth, *Zechariah's Prophetic Vision for the New World*, Olive Press, Columbia, SC, © 2002, p. 265.

Study Seven

What's Ahead for the Jews?

Every so often a verse of Scripture seems to come to the light and receives much usage, especially one which gives a good measure of encouragement to persons who are struggling with a problem in their life. Such a one is Jeremiah 29:11 which proclaims, "'For I know the plans I have for you,' declares the Lord, 'plans to prosper you and not to harm you, plans to give you hope and a future.'"

This is certainly a marvelous word from God and I can testify to how much it has encouraged me at strategic times of need in my life. While it is never wrong to appropriate a verse of Scripture for our own edification and comfort, it is often helpful to search the context in which the words were first given and to whom and for what purpose.

This is certainly the case with the verse God gave through the prophet Jeremiah. This wonderful verse we are considering was in a letter which Jeremiah sent to the leadership of the Hebrew people who had been taken captive from Jerusalem to Babylon. God had used the Babylonian King Nebuchadnezzar to bring punishment upon the Jews because they had been unwilling to listen to God and obey Him. Now they receive a letter with directions from God as to how they were to live while in the foreign land.

They were told to settle down, plant gardens, build houses and to marry and have children. In other words, carry on with life. He also told them to seek for peace and prosperity for Babylon, for they would also share in the prosperity of the land where they were living. This was a way of reminding them that one of the reasons they had been called through Abraham was to be a blessing to the other nations.

But God's words do not end there. He tells them exactly how long they will be living in Babylon and what God's expectations for them are in the future. Listen to the larger part of Scripture that surrounds our familiar verse.

This is what the Lord says, "When seventy years are completed for Babylon, I will come to you and fulfill my gracious promise to bring you back to this place. For I know the plans I have for you," declares the Lord, "plans to prosper you and not to harm you, plans to give you hope and a future. Then you will call upon me and come and pray to me, and I will listen to you. You will seek me and find me when you seek me with all your heart. I will be found by you," declares the Lord, "and I will bring you back from captivity. I will gather you from all the nations and places where I have banished you," declares the Lord, "and will bring you back to the place from which I carried you into exile" (Jeremiah 29:10-14).

This verse, which seems to have such a personal application, was originally spoken as a promise to a captive people in a foreign land, the Jews in Babylon. That makes this a most pertinent passage of Scripture for us in these tumultuous days. We are daily confronted with a world at conflict with God's people, the Jews. Here we have a prophetic word from God Himself about their future.

This promise was originally fulfilled exactly on schedule when after 70 years in Babylon, the Jews were freed by decree of the new king, Cyrus, to go back to Jerusalem and to begin to rebuild the temple. But there is a portion of their message from the Lord through Jeremiah that gives us an understanding that this prophecy is one which has a dual fulfillment. It has already been fulfilled once, but it will be so again. How do we know? The last verse above indicates that God is going to bring them back "from all the nations and places where I have banished you."

In the original fulfillment, the exiles returned from only one nation, one place. That was Babylon. However, they are also told that they are coming back from all the nations. That could only refer to what is taking place in the world today. Since the destruction of Jerusalem and the temple in A.D. 70, the Jews have been scattered over the entire world. This wonderful promise of God was not only for the Babylonian exiles, it is for the vast multitude of Jews who have been living in world-wide dispersion for well over 19 centuries.

The important concept for us to grasp is that God not only has a plan for His people, the Jews, but He has revealed many of the details of how this plan will unfold. Unfortunately, both Judaism and Christianity have either misread or have chosen to believe other than what God has clearly revealed by His prophets.

Thus, today both Israel and the world at large are shuffling about attempting to make some sense of what to do with the Jews, ever wondering what will become of these people who have been so hated by the nations and peoples of the world. When we take God at His word, however, we can discover great excitement in what God has planned and what He is bringing to pass, even in these days. John Hagee, a gifted preacher, prophecy scholar and staunch supporter of the Jewish people encourages us to do so.

> *You don't have to be carried away on the winds of false doctrine. God wants us to understand His Word, and a large portion of that Word is prophecy. God's plan has existed from the foundation of the earth. Just as God Himself does not change, His plans for the earth will not change either.*[1]

What do we find when we look at Scripture to discover what is ahead for the Jews? Interestingly, we will discover that the vast majority of end times prophetic writing has to do with the Jews. In this study, we will attempt to summarize this vast amount of material in a succinct manner that will enable us to catch the flow of the prophets' messages as they play out in the plans which God knows He has for the Jews. And when God has a plan, it will come to pass exactly as He says. We look at these long-range plans under 15 headings that will take us on a whirlwind journey that began just over a century ago and culminates with the one thousand year reign of Jesus as King upon the earth.

170

No. 1: Regathering from Dispersion

God often uses a single individual to arouse His people to begin to respond to His prophetic Word. This was certainly the case with a Hungarian-born Jew whom God gave a vision for the reestablishment of a homeland for the Jews after more than 1,900 years of dispersion. Theodor Herzl became convinced that it was necessary, at the end of the nineteenth century, for the Jews to begin to migrate to their former homeland to avoid the rampant anti-Semitism which he saw in increasing intensity around the world.

Herzl began to speak of his vision and made contact with influential people to gain support. A Wikipedia contributor summarizes how this vision began to crystallize:

> *In London's East End, a community of primarily Yiddish speaking recent Jewish immigrants, Herzl addressed a mass rally of thousands on July 12, 1896, and was received with acclaim. They granted Herzl the mandate of leadership for Zionism. Within six months this mandate had been expanded throughout Zionist Jewry. The Zionist movement grew rapidly.*[2]

The vision certainly did spread quickly. When Herzl began to speak of the Jews reclaiming their homeland, there were very few Jews then living there. The land itself was desolate and not a desirous place to live as production of food was very limited. But the people returned anyway. A half century later, so much progress had been made that Israel became a nation with approximately a half million Jews then residing in the land that had been given to their forefathers by God.

171

Why after nearly two millennia did the Jews begin to migrate back to the land that their ancestors had left? Many of them were prosperous and successful where they were living. Little was offered them in the land of Palestine except that it was the fulfillment of a dream to be restored to their ancient homeland. But, surely there is more to it than that.

Those that made *aliyah*, that is, returned to the land of Israel, most likely thought they were making the decision to do so on their own. But they were naïve. They were only responding to a greater tug upon their spirits, God Himself was diligently working to regather them from the nations to which they had been scattered. God remembered the plan He had for them and He was working to begin implementation of the plan. This plan is specifically mentioned by Nehemiah when he was still in Babylon after some of the exiles had returned to Jerusalem. How well it still describes the situation today. Nehemiah says to God,

> *"Remember the instruction you gave your servant, Moses, saying, 'If you are unfaithful, I will scatter you among the nations, but if you return to me and obey my commands, then even if your exiled people are at the farthest horizon, I will gather them from there and bring them to the place I have chosen as a dwelling for my name'"* (Nehemiah 1:8f).

When we see the Jews returning to Israel, it is a marvel of God's ability to place a word of prophecy in Scripture and then to bring it to precise fulfillment. That is what we have been witnessing for the past 120 years. Ezekiel records what God says about this same matter right after giving the prophet the vision of the valley of dry bones. In only one of many promises of coming back to the land, God says to Ezekiel,

"...say to them, 'This is what the sovereign Lord says: I will take the Israelites out of the nations where they have gone. I will gather them from all around and bring them back into their own land. I will make them one nation in the land, on the mountains of Israel. There will be one king over all of them and they will never again be two nations or be divided into two kingdoms'" (Ezekiel 37:21f).

It is very evident that the regathering is an act of God. He is demonstrating in this return that His plan is to preserve and bless Israel. His great love is demonstrated both in what He says and what He does. He declares that not only is He regathering the Jews, but He Himself will be taking care of them when they return.

"'I will bring them out from the nations and gather them from the countries, and I will bring them into their own land. I will pasture them on the mountains of Israel, in the ravines and in all the settlements in the land. I will tend them in a good pasture, and the mountain heights of Israel will be their grazing land'" (Ezekiel 34:13f).

What's the great importance of this regathering? When we study the prophecies in the Bible concerning the End-Times, we discover that God's time clock came to a stop at the time of the crucifixion of Jesus, the rejection of the Messiah whom the Father sent to bring salvation. The Church Age has been a time to proclaim salvation to the nations of the world. When that task is completed and Israel is once again in her land and functioning as a nation, then

God's time clock begins to move once again. It has not been until the middle of the last century that we have seen this take place. Elwood McQuaid speaks to the unlikely prospect of what has happened.

> *First, we are told that Israel would be cast among the nations. We need not be reminded that this is one of the best-attested facts in all of human history. For nearly 2000 years, Jews have wandered as foot-sore sojourners among often-inhospitable Gentiles. The prophecies of Israel's dispersion have been literally fulfilled.*
>
> *Next is the promise that even though the nation would be forced from its home for extended periods of time, there would always be an Israel. That Jewry has survived, as the Scriptures said it would, is certainly one of the great miracles of human history.[3]*

Not only do we marvel at the very continued existence of the Jews, we can fully expect their regathering to continue unabated until the time of the end of the Tribulation period. There are now more than six million Jews living in Israel, about one half of all the Jews in the world. Those who have not returned and are still alive at the end of the Tribulation will be gathered by God's angels and brought back to Jerusalem where they will be among the remnant who will accept Jesus as their Messiah and be saved after His coming in power and glory.

No. 2: Reborn as a Nation

There is little value, however, of being gathered together as a people if there is no organizational entity to give direction and cohesiveness to the population. It was good for the Jews to be coming back to the land, but they needed to become a nation once again. But could such a thing take place? After all, the people had not been a nation for nineteen hundred years. And the last years of their nationhood had been under the dominance of the Romans.

Surely, such a prospect seemed unlikely. But, the Jews are not just like other peoples. With only man's ability, coming back from two thousand years of non-nationhood to once again being among the nation states of the world is certainly an improbability. The Jews had lived among many peoples, being hated by most of them. They had not used Hebrew as their common language for generations. They had no recognized leadership. They had no taxes or way of raising revenue. In short, they were totally ill equipped to even think about becoming a nation.

God, however, must be put into the equation. He had allowed His chosen people to be defeated in their own nation and then scattered to the ends of the earth. Could the dream of once again residing in their own land be the vision of God's plan and purpose for these people? It is surely so. God likens this motley band of immigrants to a woman ready to give birth to a child. In the last chapter of Isaiah's word from the Lord we read these exciting words:

> *"Before she goes into labor, she gives birth; before the pains come upon her, she delivers a son. Who has ever heard of such a thing? Who has ever seen such things? Can a country be born in a day or a nation be brought forth in a moment? Yet no sooner is Zion in labor than she gives birth to her children. Do I bring to the moment of birth and not give delivery?" says the Lord* (Isaiah 66:7-9).

Here we find God setting forth exactly what would happen and what did happen in 1948. We have not the space here to detail all the background that went into Israel being born once again as a nation. But, God says that as soon as it was time for the birth, He would give the delivery. And He did, and in a single day, the nation was brought forth.

That single day was on May 14, 1948, when David Ben-Gurion stood before his fellow Jews and declared the independence of the Jewish people and the formation of a new nation by the name of Israel. The next morning, the brilliant white flag of the nation featuring two royal blue stripes, reminiscent of the prayer shawl, and the star of David was raised over Tel Aviv. God had brought His people back, planted them in their land and brought forth a nation to stand among the people of the world as testimony to His glory.

What is so important about Israel becoming a nation? Some of today's leading prophecy scholars and teachers give us good insight on this question.

With such destruction of Jerusalem, however, and the scattering of the children of Israel, their national characteristics were blurred for many centuries. It is of tremendous significance, however, that the ties which bound together the race of Israel were of such character that in our modern day the nation Israel has once gain returned to the ancient land, established itself as a political state, and is recognized as such by most of the civilized world.[4]

Had more people been reading the writings of a prophet named Ezekiel, they would not have been so surprised by the birth pangs of the nation of Israel or the regathering of Jews from all over the world to Palestine. The creation of modern Israel made possible the fulfillment of a prophecy made some twenty-five centuries before the fact: Ezekiel's foretelling of the scattering and regathering of the exiles of Israel.[5]

The spot in Tel Aviv, Israel, where David Ben Gurion proclaimed the statehood of Israel. A visit here gives a real sense of the awesome reality of the nation's rebirth against overwhelming odds.

Perry Stone lists the birth of Israel as the number one reason for believing we are living in the time of the end and gives the following rationale:

> *Therefore, consider that no end time prophecy concerning the nation of Israel could have been fulfilled before 1948! This is because Israel did not exist as a nation until May 14-15, 1948. . . .Therefore, if no end time prophecy concerning Israel could have been fulfilled until Israel was once again a nation, and we now have a sovereign nation of Israel, then that nation is a sign that we live in the time of the end.[6]*

At that point, Stone is in agreement with God. For God speaks through Isaiah once again later in the same chapter as we noted above and indicated that the birth of Israel was to be a sign to the other nations.

> *"I will set a sign among them, and I will send some of those who survive to the nations. . .that have not heard of my name or seen my glory. They will proclaim my glory among the nations"* (Isaiah 66:19).

Jesus Himself indicated that we should watch for such a sign. The disciples had asked Jesus about what sign they could look for that would signal the end of the age. One of the answers He gave them was this: "Now learn this lesson from the fig tree. As soon as its twigs get tender and its leaves come out, you know that summer is near. Even so, when you see all these things, you know that it is near, right at the door" (Matthew 24:32). But not everyone was delighted to see what God was doing.

> *Since Israel's birth, Arab nations have wanted a united front against "the Zionist entity." All have rejected Israel's right to exist and have, in fact, adopted 35 resolutions in the U.N. effectively calling for the dismantling of a Zionist (sic) [state].[7]*

The fig tree is one of the symbols used by Jesus to refer to Israel. The nation has certainly put forth evidence that it is coming to full bloom. That is, it will be resuming its role as God's instrument to bless the nations. Before that fullness comes, however, we will see Israel going through exceedingly difficult days. The point is abundantly clear. The fig tree is showing forth its leaves and God's plans for Israel are moving without fail towards their full completion.

The birth of Israel as a nation is, without doubt, the most important date on God's prophetic calendar in the past two millennia. Many of us have been privileged to live through these early days of that nation. But, in a real sense, that is only a moment. The major factors in God's amazing scheme of things are yet ahead of us. We must heed the words of Jesus to keep watch on this important sign—Israel the nation. We will be, thus, able to discern the times.

No. 3: Restored to the Land

Could the Jewish people be a nation anywhere else than in the land of the Bible? In the earlier years of the last century when the world was attempting to determine what to do with the Jews, most were admitting that they should have a land of their own. The difficulty was where that land should be. Some suggested some desolate place in central Africa. Others even proposed that they be given some barren and unpopulated area in the western part of the United States. The Jewish people would have none of that, insisting that they must be back in their ancient homeland.

They were correct, of course, not just because of their desire, but because that was what God had promised a multitude of times throughout the Bible. Which reminds us, that a basic starting point if we want to understand Bible prophecy is that we must believe the Bible strongly enough to take it literally, even when we don't understand it. Much of the turmoil in the Middle East today would dissolve if the parties believed what God has already said about specific prophetic issues.

This is especially evident in regards to Israel once again possessing the land they occupied before the Roman destruction of Jerusalem and the Temple in A.D. 70. Listen to the precision of detail as God speaks through the prophet.

"I will bring back my exiled people Israel; they will rebuild the ruined cities and live in them. They will plant vineyards and drink their wine; they will make gardens and eat their fruit. I will plant Israel in their own land never again to be uprooted from the land I have given them," says the Lord your God (Amos 9:14f).

There are some key truths here that we dare not miss. First of all, God says that He is the One who is bringing the exiles back. Secondly, He indicates that He will prosper them as they reclaim their former land which had become desolate. The third evident reality is that God says He will plant them and they will never be uprooted again. And fourthly, He indicates that this will take place in the land that has been given to them through the covenants with Abraham and his descendents.

Every one of these truths have a very pertinent place as the peace-seeking activities between Israel and her neighbors continue to dominate the news. Until the parties can agree to an accord that is in harmony with the Word of God, there will be no peace. The Scriptures do not hold forth promise that we can expect to see a workable agreement take place. Jeremiah affirms this principle with these words from the Lord:

" 'The days are coming' declares the Lord, 'when I will bring my people Israel and Judah back from captivity and

*restore them to the land I gave their forefathers to possess'
says the Lord"* (Jeremiah 30:3)

One frequent visitor to Israel shares of the change which has
come over the land since Israel has come home:

> *The transformation of the land of Israel from mosquito-
> infested swamps and barren desert to productive farms,
> vineyards and orchards is amazing. The Lord has blessed
> Israelis' hard work. One indication is the jet stream, which
> has actually shifted so that some of the former desert land
> has regular rain again.*[8]

The word "restore" is one which we of necessity must watch
for in prophetic Scripture. In many places, God promises to restore
things to the way they were in the beginning. That's what makes
prophecy so exciting. God is taking us someplace and He shares
much of what it is all about. That is why it is important to seek out
various passages of Scripture which gave a variety of facets to one
truth.

One aspect of Israel's restoration to the land is the fact of its
permanence. This has not been the case in previous returns as Walvood points out,

> *The missing ingredient in the regatherings from the
> first and second dispersions was Israel's possession of the
> land forever. This will be fulfilled in their third and final
> regathering. . . .This emphasizes an important point in the
> doctrine that the people of Israel would return to their
> land—namely, that they would return to the land not be-
> cause they deserved it but because they are the recipients of*

God's grace. Even in their apostasy God reminded them that they would be regathered.[9]

At the present time we see a partial restoration of Israel to their land. This will continue, albeit with much opposition from their neighboring nations. The complete restoration will occur only following the coming of Messiah in power and glory to end the Tribulation and defeat the nations gathered for the campaign of Armageddon. Then Israel will accept the Lordship of Yeshua and reign with Him in His kingdom. Their portion of His worldly kingdom will encompass all that territory promised to them with a forever title deed to the land.

No. 4: Resistance Over Jerusalem

"From the time Jerusalem became the capital of Israel in 1004 B.C., no less than 69 battles have been fought over the city."[10] With the reality that circumstances seem reluctant to change, it is a certainty that we will continue to see conflict over the city which God calls His dwelling place on earth.

> *This is what the Lord says, "I will return to Zion and dwell in Jerusalem. Then Jerusalem will be called the City of Truth, and the mountain of the Lord will be called the Holy Mountain"* (Zechariah 8:3).

The fact that today we are seeing an ongoing struggle over the city of Jerusalem and the Temple Mount is, therefore, not surprising. The city is a holy site to three major religions or faiths. The Jewish people have been there since the day God commanded

Abraham to take his son Isaac and offer him as a sacrifice. Among any thinking people, there can be no question of Israel's right to the city. Christianity's connection to Jerusalem comes because of our Jewish background and heritage.

The claim of Islam to Jerusalem as its third most holy city, however, is without foundation. The Muslim faith was not established until the seventh century A.D.. The Koran makes not one mention of Jerusalem. The Muslim claim is of recent fabrication.

The conflict over Jerusalem will continue until we move into a new end times scenario which will take us to the return of Jesus as Messiah and conqueror of all the armies of the world who will be attempting to bring final annihilation to the Jewish people.

Mike Evans, a most perceptive writer about the current world situation in light of Bible prophecy, emphasizes the importance of Jerusalem.

This city is the centerpiece of Bible prophecy, and it is to this place that Messiah will return. Jesus will not return to a Muslim city. Not because he is prejudiced against them, but because he promised two thousand years ago that Jerusalem would be trodden down by the Gentiles until the time of the Gentiles was over (Luke 21:24). Through the centuries this prophecy has stood as an immovable landmark by which we may gauge the often confusing events of Jewish history.

Today Jerusalem remains the capital of Israel, the very heart of the nation. . .the City of David has always had a special destiny and a unique calling before God.[11]

View of Muslim Dome of the Rock with Jewish Western Wall in foreground illustrates the continuing conflict over control of Jerusalem and specifically the Temple Mount area .

As one writer has said, "Jerusalem was the magnet that pulled the Jewish people back to their ancestral homeland well before the creation of the State of Israel."[12]

Jerusalem is at the very heart of everything Jewish. Through all the years of the dispersion, every Passover meal concluded with the excited shouting of the words, "Next year, Jerusalem!" And, indeed, each year sees more and more Jews partaking of the Seder meal in Israel without yet knowing the Lamb of God to which the ceremony points.

So while, in a technical sense, Jerusalem is now under the control of Israel, management of the Temple Mount, the spiritual focus of the city, is still in the hands of those outside the family of Judaism. The battle for the city is not over. We will see it continuing until the time of the end, as Bible prophecy clearly indicates.

Evans has written, "In Hebrew the city is *Yerushalayim*. The name literally means 'city of peace' from the words *yerah* (city)

---

and *shalom* (peace)—a rather ironic designation given the amount of violence and bloodshed it has seen through the centuries.[13]

We are told in Psalm 122:6 that we are to "Pray for the peace of Jerusalem: May those who love you be secure. May there be peace within your walls and security within your citadels." When we pray thus, we do so knowing that longed-for peace will only be achieved when the Prince of Peace returns and establishes his Kingdom of peace. Let us not fall into the error of believing that peace will come to the city of Jerusalem and the Nation of Israel through the efforts of human peace makers. Israel will continue to find resistance to their full control of their capital city.

While the immediate future looks bleak, the Bible gives us a final word which is extremely encouraging and points to the reality of God having a plan which will come to pass.

In the last days the mountain of the Lord's temple will be established as chief among the mountains; it will be raised above the hills, and all nations will stream to it.

Many peoples will come and say, "Come, let us go up to the mountain of the Lord, to the house of the God of Jacob. He will teach us his ways, so that we may walk in his paths" (Isaiah 2:3f).

No. 5: Rebuffing Attacks of Neighbor Nations

Before Israel gets to the place which Isaiah describes, they will be continually dogged with attacks from those countries which surround them and, ultimately, from all the world's nations. It is not a pleasant picture to contemplate. The Scriptures are clear that this is so, however, and it is a good thing for us to be aware of what is ahead for this little nation which has been an ally of the United States since its birth, even though that relationship seems to be in a deteriorating mode in recent days.

Let's review how Israel has had to defend itself in the two-thirds of a century since it declared itself a nation.

The neighbors of the new Jewish state were determined that Israel would not be allowed to survive. On the day following their declaration as a nation, they were attacked from all sides by well-equipped Muslim nations, five in all. It was what was designed to be a war of annihilation, but something happened. Though outnumbered by more than 100 to one and with little training and almost no weaponry, the new State of Israel prevailed, shocking not just their Muslim attackers, but the entire world. Hal Lindsey summarizes as follows:

> *The land of Israel become the land of the Jews, by miracle, if you please. Their victory is inexplicable apart from the unseen intervention of the Hand of God. God has a plan for the last days. A restored land of Israel, homeland to the Jewish people, is the key element in His plan, and the very existence of Israel bears testimony to it.*[14]

But that was not the end of the aggression. In 1967, the struggling young nation was attacked by Jordan with hopes of capturing the portion of Jerusalem which they did not control. They were joined by Egypt, Iraq and Syria. Of course, the ultimate goal would have been to totally drive out the Jews. But once again, Israel prevailed against great odds, not only withstanding the invading forces but also to greatly expand the land area of Israel. They were able to capture the west bank, the Golan Heights, the Gaza Strip and all of the Sinai peninsula.

They now had borders which they could defend. But that victory has been the cause of the continuing struggles of these lands and are very much so today. That was all accomplished in six days—the Six Day War.

Trouble came once again in 1973 when Egypt and Syria led a coalition of states in a surprise attack on Yom Kippur in October. The goal of the invaders was to retake territory lost to Israel in the Six Day Way. However, Israel once again prevailed over the Arabs and no territory changed hands.

Those were the major wars against Israel since Statehood, but there has been continual troubles during the entire time. In the north, there has been severe conflicts with guerilla forces in Lebanon, primarily Hezbollah and Palestinian groups. Gaza was turned over to the Palestinians in 2005 with a total Israeli withdrawal as an overture of peace. Since then, tens of thousands of rockets have been fired into Israel with many skirmishes taking place between the two areas.

There have also been two intifadas declared by the Palestinians. These are characterized by a variety of uprisings, violence and suicide bombings throughout Israel. So, since its beginning, Israel as a state has been besieged. The neighbors of the new Jewish state have been anything but neighborly.

. . .although Muslims disagree on many things, often to the point of warring against one another, there is almost universal agreement on one subject: the existence of the State of Israel and a negative attitude toward the Jewish people. Another major point of conflict for mainstream

187

Muslims is the Western "Christian" influence, which is viewed as a corrupting force in the Islamic world.[15]

What can we expect in the future? The simple answer is "more of the same." The Bible also teaches that Israel will have more major conflicts. These are worthy of lengthy discussion, but we will only comment on them briefly at this point.

The first possible future war is one which is often not considered. It is known as the Psalm 83 war and is based on this Scripture:

O God, do not keep silent; be not quiet, O God, be not still. See how your enemies are astir, how your foes rear their heads. With cunning they conspire against your people; they plot against those you cherish. "Come," they say, "let us destroy them as a nation, that the name of Israel be remembered no more."

With one mind they plot together; they form an alliance against you—the tents of Edom and the Ishmaelites, of Moab and the Hagrites, Gebal, Ammon and Amalek, Philistia, and the people of Tyre (Psalm 83:1-8).

Notice how similar the words of Israel's enemies today sound to those of the day when Asaph penned the Psalm. The words to destroy Israel and the memory of their name forever could have come straight from the leaders of Iran and Hamas, the terrorist organization which controls the Gaza strip. This coalition of nations could well be the next major attack on the nation of Israel. It will consist of all the nations which are immediate neighbors of Israel: Jordan, Egypt, Lebanon, Syria and those Palestinians living in the West Bank and Gaza Strip.

We have neither mention in the Psalm of the outcome of this war nor idea of any precise placement of it in God's prophetic

188

plan. But we do hear the Psalmist concluding with the assurance that what takes place will "Let them know that you, whose name is the Lord—that you alone are the Most High over all the earth" (Psalm 83:18).

If you would like to get some good study information on Psalm 83, I would recommend you find material from Bill Salus. He has excellent insights on this topic.

A much more well-known attack on Israel is that which we find in Ezekiel's record of God's prophetic word. Note the detail with which God describes this coming massive invasion:

> *The Word of God came to me: "Son of man, set your face against Gog, of the land of Magog, the chief prince of Meshech and Tubal; prophesy against him and say: 'This is what the sovereign Lord says: I am against you, O Gog, chief prince of Meshech and Tubal. I will turn you around, put hooks in your jaws and bring you out with your whole army—your horses, your horsemen fully armed, and a great horde with large and small shields, all of them brandishing their swords. Persia, Cush and Put will be with them, all with shields and helmets, also Gomer with all its troops, and Beth Togarmah from the far north with all its troops—the many nations with you.*
>
> *"'After many days you will be called to arms. In future years you will invade a land that has recovered from war, whose people were gathered from many nations to the mountains of Israel, which had long been desolate. They have been brought out from the nations, and now all of them live in safety. You and all your troops and the many nations with you will go up, advancing like a storm; you will be like a cloud covering the land'"* (Ezekiel 38:1-6, 8-9).

When will this invasion take place. Some interpreters think that this is a reference to the Campaign of Armageddon, but that seems highly unlikely as God says Israel will be living in safety. That cannot describe life during the Tribulation, at whose conclusion Armageddon comes. So it must come near the beginning of the Tribulation period, perhaps soon after Israel and other nations sign a covenant with the antichrist which will give God's people, the Jews, a sense of peace and security.

There are an abundance of good commentaries on the Gog and Magog battle so we will not take the space to reiterate much of it here. McCall and Levitt have a summary paragraph that succinctly tells the story:

> . .the dynamic 38th and 39th chapters of Ezekiel present the scenario of a great power to the extreme north of Israel mounting a massive invasion "in the last days." The great power is cryptically referred to as "Magog," and it forms a coalition with several other specific nations located in Eastern Europe, Persia, Ethiopia, and Libya for the purpose of that attack on Israel. The invading powers will be annihilated—thoroughly destroyed—and Israel will emerge from the conflict victorious.[16]

Please take note of a couple of important facts about this battle. It cannot be equated with Psalm 83 because the listing of nations is quite precise and they are absolutely a different list in each case. Neither can it be a part of Armageddon as that campaign will involve all nations of the world, whereas Gog and Magog is limited to specific countries.

God makes it quite clear that the battle will not belong to Israel and the IDF (Israel Defense Force) troops. It will be God's own doing that brings this war to a conclusion. He explains His priority in showing forth His holiness.

"I will execute judgment upon him with plague and bloodshed; I will pour down torrents of rain, hailstones and burning sulfur on him and on his troops and on the many nations with him. And so I will show my greatness and my holiness, and I will make myself known in the sight of many nations" (Ezekiel 38:22f).

This battle will have major consequences for Israel. It will once again enlarge their borders. Along with the covenant the nation will sign with the Antichrist, the nation will be in a time of peace and security never before known. This will set them up for the greatest conflict of all, the world-wide convergence of military forces to come against Israel in the frightening campaign of annihilation, which we commonly refer to as Armageddon.

We find some detail about this gigantic campaign in the message which God gave to Zechariah.

This is the word of the Lord concerning Israel. The Lord, who stretches out the heavens, who lays the foundation of the earth, and who forms the spirit of man within him, declares: "I am going to make Jerusalem a cup that sends all the surrounding peoples reeling. Judah will be besieged as well as Jerusalem. On that day, when all the nations of the earth are gathered against her I will make Jerusalem an immovable rock for all the nations. All who try to move it will injure themselves."

A day of the Lord is coming when your plunder will be divided among you. I will gather all the nations to Jerusalem to fight against it; the city will be captured, the houses ransacked, and the women raped. Half of the city will go

into exile, but the rest of the people will not be taken from the city.
Then the Lord will go out and fight against those nations, as he fights in the day of battle (Zechariah 12:1-3, 14:1-3).

For nearly four milennia the nations of the world have sought to subdue Jerusalem and the Israelites. Oftentimes they were successful, but the Jews kept returning. There is something about being in the land which God has given them that is an essential part of their DNA as a people. Now they are back in the land once again, but this time with a promise that they will never again be uprooted no matter what level of conflict they have to endure. The years ahead will be terrible ones for the Jewish people. Jesus said of this time in Matthew 24:21, "For then there will be great distress, unequaled from the beginning of the world until now—and never to be equaled again."

> *But in this final hour of terrible conflict, something miraculous will transpire among the people of Israel. Pressed to the wall, the Promised Land torn apart in vicious war, their historic fears of national annihilation coming to reality before their eyes, the Jews turn to God. They have always done this, but in this case they turn to their Messiah—at Last!*
>
> *It will be the greatest spiritual awakening in all of history, as the Jews come to Christ by the millions. It will be a true Day of Atonement in Israel.*[17]

We know from God's Word that Israel is going to experience the most horrific times imaginable in the year's ahead. But the end is in sight. It could be as few as seven years until the prophecy of the Apostle Paul is realized: "And so all Israel will be saved, as it is written: 'The deliverer will come from Zion; he will turn godlessness away from Jacob'" (Romans 11:26).

No. 6: Removal of Christian Believers

The dramatic event for which most alert Christians look and long for is the Rapture of the Bride of Christ. This is a key prophetic doctrine for followers of Jesus, but it has great significance for the Jews as well. The clearest Scripture telling of this wonderful experience is found in Paul's writings:

> *According to the Lord's own word, we tell you that we who are still alive, who are left till the coming of the Lord will certainly not precede those who have fallen asleep. For the Lord himself will come down from heaven, with a loud command, with the voice of the archangel and with the trumpet call of God, and the dead in Christ will rise first. After that, we who are still alive and are left will be caught up with them in the clouds to meet the Lord in the air. And so we will be with the Lord forever* (1 Thessalonians 4:15-17).

We will not discuss here the implications of the Rapture as they are covered quite well in Study Three. What we want to think of briefly at this point is the influence that the Rapture will have on the Jewish people. Arno Froese reminds us that the Rapture of living believers from the earth is going to have a profound impact; it will be a great turning point in Bible prophecy.

> *We must not overlook that there will be a terrific void on earth when the Church of Jesus Christ has been rap-*

193

tured. The light of the world will be gone, the salt of the earth will have disappeared and countless angels, which minister to the saints, as Hebrews 1:14 indicates, will have disappeared: "Are they not all ministering spirits, sent forth to minister for them who shall be heirs of salvation?" The time for the Great Tribulation will have begun![18]

There is certainly a good bit of difference of opinion about when the Rapture takes place and how it relates to the Tribulation period. A most significant truth is given us by the Apostle Paul. In speaking about when the Antichrist will be revealed, Paul says that that there is One who is holding him back: "For the secret power of lawlessness is already at work; but the one who now holds it back will continue to do so till he is taken out of the way. And then the lawless one will be revealed" (2 Thessalonians 2:7).

This one whom Paul refers to is referred to in the King James Version as the restrainer, as a person with the pronoun *he*. Many scholars believe that this is a clear reference to the Holy Spirit whose work through committed Christians is holding back the Tribulation which will begin when Antichrist is free to begin his dastardly work and signs a covenant with Israel and other nations which he has no intent of keeping. McQuaid reminds us of the value of peace agreements to the Islamic world as he refers back to the days of Yasser Arafat.

Throughout much of his terrorist career, Yasser Arafat has promised that if a Palestinian state were to become a reality, it would be only the first stage in the overall program to destroy Israel. This tactic of making peace when you are too weak to defeat your enemy is a staple in the Islamic system. Treaties mean nothing when Muslims become strong enough to defeat their foes.

But we must remember that these people and their companions in error are committed wholly to the concept of killing Jews, destroying Israel, and subjugating the world—all in the name of Allah and Jihad. Therefore we are dealing with people who by their own admission cannot change their goals—only their tactics.[19]

The Spirit has many ministries that are fulfilled through Christian believers. One of them is to assist in the restraining of evil. When the Bride is taken to heaven by the Bridegroom, the restraining influence of the Spirit will go with them. The Spirit will still be active on earth in his other ministries but the lack of restraint will unleash a deluge of evil that the Jews will be left to face. Mark Hitchcock makes a great point of this:

Amazingly, this present age in which we live is described as the time or age of restraint. There is something or someone who is restraining or holding back the full blast of evil that is to come when the Antichrist is unleashed. Think about it for a moment. If this evil day is which we now live is described as the time of restraint, what in the world will it be like when the restraint is removed?. . .It will be like removing a dam from a lake—evil will overflow this world, swamping everything in its path.[20]

That is why the Rapture is important to the Jews. It will open the door for massive evil to be let loose in the world and the Jewish people, their nation, their city of Jerusalem and the God called who called them to be His people will be the focus of much of the wrath.

No. 7: Reach a Treaty with Antichrist

Who is the Antichrist? That's the question that has fascinated persons for generations. Even those who have no real interest in Bible prophecy seem driven to know the identity of this nefarious character. So in answer, the most monstrous and vile person identifiable is usually put forth as the logical one to fulfill this role. But as time passes and the person dies without taking the role of antichrist, it becomes necessary to look for another.

Perhaps it would be better to follow the Biblical pattern. We are told that the antichrist will be revealed in the proper time, therefore, it is useless for us to attempt any identification on our own. The other Biblical perspective worthy of note is that it is far more productive to focus on his nature and the things that he does, rather than what his name might be. No matter what name he holds, his nature will be thoroughly Satanic.

We cannot forget that, from the beginning, the Promised Seed was destined to destroy the seed of the serpent. The serpent, in turn, sought to destroy Him and will pursue this course until the bitter end. We also cannot forget that the first man to oppose the Seed and the Blood of the Lamb was also the first man to be stigmatized with a mark that identified him as all that is unholy and blasphemous. In the end, the anti-Messiah will exhibit the same traits as Cain. Like Cain, he will epitomize the very nature of the serpent, and will be empowered to enforce the consequences of that nature upon all to the degree that mankind will be compelled to be stigmatized with his satanic and blasphemous mark (Rev. 13:16-17).[21]

It is most appropriate, however, to reflect upon the subject of the area from which the antichrist will arise. For most of the recent two centuries just past, the idea taught by most prophecy teachers was that the antichrist would arise out of the reconstituted Roman Empire and would therefore come from Europe, likely from Rome itself. This view is referenced by John Hagee in the quote on the next page.

In very recent years, however, many have come to think of the other portion of the Roman Empire, that of the Eastern leg, which was centered in Constantinople. This idea has doubtless been fueled by the ever strengthening rise of Islam in the Middle East. Bill Cloud speaks for many in today's Bible prophecy scene who are now expecting the antichrist to be a Muslim when he is revealed.

> *I am convinced that all the evidence—that which was revealed in the beginning through Cain and his seed, and that which is contained in the writings of Daniel and all the other prophets—clearly points to the Islamic world as the sea of people from which the anti-Messiah shall arise.*
>
> *I do not stand alone in this diagnosis. Many others have recently arrived at the same conclusion. I was somewhat excited to learn that the ancient Jewish commentator Ibn Ezra (1089-11264) wholeheartedly believed that the last kingdom would be as Islamic one.*[22]

Our basic reference for the covenant or treaty to be signed is given to us by Daniel at God's instruction. He tells us just the bare-bones details as a part of the revealing the seventy "Sevens" and says:

197

*"He will confirm a covenant with many for one 'seven.'
In the middle of the 'seven' he will put an end to sacrifice
and offering. And on a wing of the temple he will set up an
abomination that causes desolation until the end that is
decreed is poured out on him"* (Daniel 9:27).

Daniel's seventy weeks, which actually refer to seventy weeks of years, or 490 years, is the key to all Bible prophecy from the time of the end of the exile of the Jews in Babylon to the coming of Messiah in power and great glory at the end of the tribulation. Sixty-nine of those weeks have already passed and we now await the beginning of the final "week" which will consist of the seven years just preceding the Messiah's coming.

The importance of the covenant which Antichrist negotiates with Israel and other nations is that it is the trigger which will set in motion Daniel's final week. The following is an excellent summary by Hagee of just how this all plays out:

> *The seventieth "week" will begin when the church age ends, namely, with the Rapture. Then will come the Antichrist, making a covenant with the Jewish people. He will offer peace and a guarantee of safety against a threatening Roman domination that comes in the form of the federated states of Europe. . . .it is clear that seven literal years is the period of the seventieth 'week.' So after three and one-half years, the Antichrist will betray Israel and come to attack her. The great battle of Armageddon will ensue. Christ Himself will return (the Second Coming) to crush the Antichrist and all his forces.*[23]

Since we have this knowledge that the antichrist will turn his back on Israel, we have to ask why Israel will sign the agreement in the first place. They will probably have just come through the battle of Gog and Magog and are exhausted and in need of some assurance of peace and security for the future. Plus, they most likely will be granted permission in the agreement to begin construction of the next Temple on the temple mount in Jerusalem which at present is impossible with the political situation as it currently stands with the Palestinians and the Jordanians.

Michael Evans has thoughts on the rationale for Israel to enter into a covenant relationship with the new global leader and what practical implications it may hold for the Jewish people:

> At first everything will appear to be going well. The centuries of armed tension will be relieved. By the peace imposed through the power of the Antichrist, Israel will be able to turn its full attention to the development of the country and its resources and will prosper as never before. The rebuilding of the Temple in Jerusalem and the resumption of sacrifices and oblations will even be permitted.
>
> But just when peace seems to have come for Israel, it will be taken from her. After three and one-half years, the Antichrist will break his treaty with Israel.[24]

While we do not know the precise details of the agreement, it is obviously a key event in the scheme of Bible prophecy as we can see the rapid unfolding of succeeding events which take place during the seven-year Tribulation period. Thus, for the Jews it will be a turning point following which they will be thrust into the final years of involvement in the plans which God has planned for their ultimate salvation.

No. 8: Rebuilding the Temple

No Jewish Temple has stood in Jerusalem since the last one was destroyed by the Romans in 70 A.D. Why after nearly two thousand years is there a deep desire to begin the building of a Temple on the ancient Temple Mount? Surely, the Jews have gotten used to being without their Temple after all these centuries. But, to say that, indicates a wholesale lack of understanding of what the Temple means to Jewish life and culture.

Randall Price has comments that may help us at this point:

> *However, if God has a future for the nation of Israel in His plan, and that plan is to be realized in the same place as it was in the past, then the Temple as a prominent symbol of that nation's past failure, should be expected to be a part of its future restoration. This indicates that God has had and still has a purpose for the Temple. . . .And what exactly is God's purpose for the Temple? A good place to begin is to look at God's plan for the Temple as first revealed to Moses.*[25]

The Hebrews had not been long gone from Egypt when God assembled them at Mt. Sinai. There they received the Ten Commandments, instructions for observing a series of solemn assemblies each year as well as instructions to build a place to represent God's presence with His people. Two verses given to Moses clearly spell out God's intent: "Then have them make a sanctuary for me, and I will dwell among them. Make this tabernacle and all its furnishings exactly like the pattern I will show you" (Exodus 25:8f).

The wilderness tabernacle was, of course, a far cry from the Temple in Jerusalem. But it served the purpose of being a physical reminder of God's presence and His laws and was a forerunner of the Temple. Later God commanded that the Temple was to be built by David's son Solomon and when it was completed, God filled the place with His overwhelming Shekinah glory. And it has been the focus, not only of Jewish worship, but of Jewish life itself ever since. Even when the people are not serving God with faith, the Temple has been a constant reminder of God's call upon them as a special people.

So it is very logical that, as they have regathered in the land and have been restored to nationhood, they should be looking forward to the day when their Temple would once again stand upon the holy mountain of God.

It has been my privilege

The author, right, in front of the Menorah for the new Temple in Jerusalem. With him is prophecy teacher Gary Fisher, left, and an Israeli Christian,

to visit the Temple Institute in Jerusalem and see the readiness for rebuilding which has been taking place. All of the Temple equipment is made and waiting. The priestly vestments are in place anticipating the day when worship and sacrifice will again be offered on the mountain top where Abraham brought his son Isaac as a sacrifice. Building materials, including two large cornerstones, are prepared and stored in anticipation of the time when permission to begin rebuilding is sounded. Standing in a prominent area in the Jewish Quarter not far from the Temple Mount is the golden menorah silently waiting for its move to the sanctuary of the Temple. There is therefore, not only a desire to see a Temple once again standing in its place in Jerusalem, but every preparation that can be made has been made for its erection and use by the Jewish people, including the training of Temple priests. It may well be that the one thing that will bring the possibility of this vital aspect of Jewish life to reality is the coming agreement signed with the Antichrist. Then the long awaited day may be very close for this function of life to be restored.

> *The Temple, therefore governed the life of the Jew. Jewish life was lived in view of the festivals, the pilgrimages, the sacrificial rites, and Torah reading and study, all of which centered on the Temple. . . .The establishment of the synagogue enabled Judaism to absorb the blow of the second temple's destruction without collapsing, but it was never meant to replace the function of the Temple in the life and faith of the Jewish people. The synagogue is only a gathering place for the community for liturgical purposes, but the Temple was "God's house," in which His presence dwelt, and which His priests attended on behalf of His people.[26]*

No. 9: Retribution Through the Tribulation

The greatest outpouring of God's wrath upon mankind ever to take place is ahead of us. We find the description of life during that time of unbelievable trouble for mankind spelled out in rather specific detail in the book of Revelation. God's displeasure, both with

Israel's failure to follow His way for them to be a blessing for the nations and to receive Jesus as their Messiah and the nations that have chosen to live in sin and degradation rather than receive His offer of salvation in Jesus, will be poured out upon the world in the form of God's great wrath for a period of seven years.

God foretold exactly what this end times scenario would look like through the words of the Old Testament prophets. Listen to the incredible harsh sentence the Lord proclaims:

> *Go, my people, enter your rooms and shut the doors behind you; hide yourselves for a little while until his wrath has passed by. See, the Lord is coming out of his dwelling to punish the people of the earth for their sins* (Isaiah 26:20f).
>
> *"'How awful that day will be! None will be like it. It will be a time of trouble for Jacob, but he will be saved out of it.'"*
> *See the storm of the Lord will burst out in wrath, a driving wind swirling down on the heads of the wicked. The fierce anger of the Lord will not turn back until he fully accomplishes the purposes of his heart* (Jeremiah 30:7, 23f).
>
> *"There will be a time of distress such as has not happened from the beginning of nations until then"* (Daniel 12:1b).

These are indeed terrible sounding descriptions of what the Tribulation period will be like. But, perhaps the most graphic terminology of all is that which God spoke through the prophet Zephaniah.

> *"The great day of the Lord is near—near and coming quickly. Listen! The cry on the day of the Lord will be bitter, the shouting of the warrior there. That day will be a day of wrath, a day of distress and anguish, a day of trouble and ruin, a day of darkness and gloom, a day of clouds and blackness, a day of trumpet and battle cry against the fortified cities and against the corner towers. I will bring distress on the people and they will walk like blind men, because they have sinned against the Lord. Their blood will be poured out like dust and their entrails like filth. Neither their silver nor their gold will be able to save them on the day of the Lord's wrath"* (1:14-18a).

This is not a time which anyone would desire to go through. But the God of justice will bring His wrath to bear upon sin and unrighteousness for all the peoples of the world. I believe that those who are true believers in Jesus and have received Him as Savior and Lord, including believing Jews, will be spared from going through that dreadful experience. The bulk of the Jewish people, however, will go through this terrible time. The anger of the other nations will be poured out against them. We read in the prophets that only one-third of the Jews will survive the Tribulation. The retribution for failing to receive God's offer of salvation is indeed severe.

God, however, has a plan and purpose for the Tribulation period. John Hagee notes four of these purposes:

> *Why does God allow this time of trouble? There are several purposes, and the first one is to bring Israel to the place where she will recognize Jesus Christ as the Messiah.*
>
> *A second purpose of the Tribulation is to judge the Gentile nations for their efforts to exterminate the nation of*

Israel.

*A third purpose of the Tribulation is to allow a **Christ-**
rejecting world to personally experience the sorrow
and suffering created by Satan's evil empire.

A fourth purpose for the Tribulation is for God's
wrath to be poured out on all who have rejected the
gospel.[27]

While this time will be disastrous for the Jews from the human
point of view, it does result in the achievement of God's purpose
for them. The Apostle Paul tell us what happens to the surviving
remnant at the conclusion of the Tribulation, "And so all Israel will
be saved, as it is written: 'The deliverer will come from Zion; he
will turn godlessness away from Jacob'" (Romans 11:26).

No. 10: Return to the Lord

"East is East and West is West, and never the twain shall meet."
This line from Rudyard Kipling pretty well expresses the attitude of
most of the world: Jews are Jews and Christians are Christians and
never the two shall meet. These skeptics include most Jews and
Christians, sorry to say. But, that is not what the Word of God says.
While the gap seems quite wide, as it has since Jesus first came on
the scene, God has a plan that will bring the two together.

Our problem is that we get irritated at how long God takes to
accomplish His plan. In teaching of the coming Day of the Lord,
the Apostle Peter reminds us of a prophetic truth we must keep in
mind:

> *But do not forget this one thing, dear friends: With the Lord a day is like a thousand years, and a thousand years are like a day. The Lord is not slow in keeping his promise, as some understand slowness. He is patient with you, not wanting anyone to perish, but everyone to come to repentance* (2 Peter 3:8f).

God called Abraham to begin a family who would serve and worship Him. The reality of that has been intermittent, with more often than not the people failing miserably in their relationship to Him. But, God never has given up on His people, the Jews. And as we face the end-times we realize that God is going to see His plan for them become reality. While we may not grasp all the detail of Israel's salvation, we can be certain that what God has said will come to pass.

> *In that day the Root of Jesse will stand as a banner for the peoples; the nations will rally to him, and his place of rest will be glorious. In that day the Lord will reach out his hand a second time to reclaim the remnant that is left of his people. . .*
> *In that day you will say: "I will praise you, O Lord. Although you were angry with me, your anger has turned away and you have comforted me. Surely God is my salvation; I will trust and not be afraid. The Lord, the Lord, is my strength and my song; he has become my salvation." With joy you will draw water from the wells of salvation* (Isaiah 11:10f, 12:1-3).

The Bible clearly indicates that the final gathering of the remnant of the Jews will all be brought to Jerusalem at God's direction and there come to accept Jesus as their longed for Messiah. For a discussion of the framework of those days, see the material on the fall feasts in Study Four on "Meeting Jesus in the Feasts of God."

But what will cause the Jews to finally look to Jesus and turn to Him in saving faith. It is really not their own doing, but God giving them a new ability to see and believe:

> *"And I will pour out on the house of David and the inhabitants of Jerusalem a spirit of grace and supplication. They will look on me, the one they have pierced, and mourn for him as one mourns for an only child, and grieve bitterly for him as one grieves for a firstborn son"* (Zechariah 12:10)

Many persons have been concerned about how Israel will be saved. Will it be through a system of sacrifice or obedience to the law? Absolutely not! The Jews will come to Jesus just like every other believer. "On that day a fountain will be opened to the house of David and the inhabitants of Jerusalem, to cleanse them from sin and impurity" (Zechariah 13:1). The fountain, of course, is the fountain filled with the blood of the Lamb of God shed at Calvary. This is why it is important for Christians to pray for and to support the Jewish people. At the end, after the horrors of the Tribulation period, those in the surviving remnant are going to find that all they have hoped for in a Messiah is in the person of *Yeshua ha Mashiach*, Jesus the Christ. Jews and Christians will be united in Jesus, whose Greek and Jewish titles, Christ and Messiah, both mean "the anointed One."

No. 11: Regeneration by the Lord

What really happens when the Jews turn to Jesus at the end of the Tribulation? There are some who teach that the event which Paul describes as "All Israel will be saved" refers only to their deliverance from their enemies. That certainly will be accomplished when Jesus brings the campaign of Armageddon to an abrupt conclusion with just a word from His mouth.

But something else takes place that is exceedingly significant. What we read in the prophets is about not just a turning to the Lord for military deliverance. We read of a deeply moving spiritual regeneration that will take place. Listen to these words; can they refer to anything other than spiritually becoming new people by the grace of the Lord?

Who is a God like you, who pardons sin and forgives the transgression of the remnant of his inheritance? You do not stay angry forever but delight to show mercy. You will again have compassion on us; you will tread our sins underfoot and hurl all our iniquities into the depths of the sea. You will be true to Jacob, and show mercy to Abraham, as you pledged on oath to our fathers in days long ago (Micah 7:18-20).

These verses referring to the "remnant" obviously are speaking of those Jews who remain alive at the end of the Tribulation. The action of God is honoring the oath made to **Abraham and his descendents**. The compassion of God gets rid of sin and iniquities. It can't really be much more clear than that. Israel comes to a time of spiritual regeneration as well as military deliverance. Ice and Price capsulize what takes place.

> *Jesus taught that His return to the earth would include delivering Israel from the fury of the Gentile nations of the world in what is known as the battle of Armageddon. At this time, Jesus declared that He would "send forth His angels with a great trumpet and they [would] gather together His elect [the Jews] from the four winds, from one end of the sky to the other"* (Matthew 24:312 clarification added).
>
> *Shortly before the Messiah's coming, the Jews will experience a true spiritual revival, a rebirth"* (*Ezekiel 37:14*). *Realizing that Jesus is their promised Messiah, they will turn to Him* (*Zechariah 12:10*). *. . . .Perhaps it will be Israel's realization that they have followed a false Messiah [the Antichrist] that will open their eyes to the fact that Jesus of Nazareth really is the one spoken of by their own prophet, Zechariah.*[28]

Ezekiel describes further what spiritual change comes to the Jews as they look to Jesus in faith:

> *"'For I will take you out of the nations; I will gather you from all the countries and bring you back into your own land. I will sprinkle clean water on you, and you will be clean; I will cleanse you from all your impurities and from all your idols. I will give you a new heart and put a new spirit in you; I will remove from you your heart of stone and give you a heart of flesh. And I will put my Spirit in you and move you to follow my decrees and be careful to keep my laws. You will live in the land I gave your forefathers; you will be my people, and I will be your God'"* (Ezekiel 36:24-28).

Thus, God makes it indisputably clear that the remnant of the Jews are going to be new people in Yeshua. Every Jew who turns to the Messiah in repentance and faith will have the same experience of salvation as every person who comes to Jesus before him. As Peter preached to the Jews right after Pentecost, "Salvation is found in no one else, for there is no other name under heaven given to men by which we must be saved" (Acts 4:12).

No. 12: Regrafted Into the Olive Tree

The Apostle Paul used the analogy of an olive tree when writing to the Roman believers about the relationship of Christians to their Jewish roots. The olive tree is one of three living things which are symbolic of the Jews in the Bible; the others being the fig tree, which we spoke of earlier in the chapter, and the vine. Grasp what Paul is saying:

> *If some of the branches have been broken off, and you, though a wild olive shoot, have been grafted in among the others and now share in the nourishing sap from the olive root, do not boast over those branches. If you do, consider this: You do not support the root, but the root supports you. You will say then, "Branches were broken off so that I could be grafted in." Granted. But they were broken off because of unbelief, and you stand by faith.*
> *And if they [the Jews] do not persist in unbelief, they will be grafted in, for God is able to graft them in again. After all, if you were cut out of an olive tree that is wild by nature, and contrary to nature were grafted into a culti-vated olive tree, how much more readily will these, the*

natural branches, be grafted into their own olive tree
(Romans 11:17-20, 22-24, clarification added).

The issue which Paul is addressing here is whether Israel has been replaced by the Christian Church. His answer is a resounding negative one. As believers in Jesus the Messiah, those outside the Jewish people, have been invited to become a part of God's ultimate plan for the redemption of mankind. Thus, Gentile believers, wild olive branches, are grafted onto the natural olive tree of Judaism.

But, the grafted in branches do not replace the original trunk and root of the natural tree. Those natural branches were broken off, said Paul, because of unbelief. But, if they did not persist in their unbelief, in other words, if they began to believe, they would be restored to the natural olive tree. And it would not be difficult for God to do so.

In other words, whenever the Jewish nation comes to a point of faith and belief in Messiah, they will be restored to the Lord, as we noted in the previous topic. This means that once more the Jews would be in a position to receive God's blessings and be used of Him to be a blessing to the nations. Wilber Dayton's commentary may help us understand this concept. Speaking of Israel as the olive tree he says,

> *So much value is built into her by centuries of cultivation that the figure is developed of grafting in wild branches (Gentiles) instead of uprooting the old tree and replacing it with a new wild tree. Legitimate Judaism (scriptural and obedient) is deeply rooted in God and truth. Perverted Judaism is then pruned away, while the root and trunk are saved on which to continue the Hebrew-Christian*

faith, whether by natural or grafted branches. Israel may come or go as individuals. The tree goes on.[29]

Thus, the great experience of the Jews, after meeting Jesus and receiving Him as their Savior and being restored to God, will be to be regrafted into the natural olive tree of Judaism. The calling, promises and covenants of God will once again be theirs. It was God's sternness, as Paul says, that caused them to be broken off. But it is also His kindness and grace which have ever stood ready to graft them once again into the fellowship of His Chosen People.

No. 13: Resurrection of Old Testament Jewish Saints

There does not seem to be a strong belief in the resurrection of the body widely expressed in the Old Testament. Job, however, did catch a glimpse of such a doctrine and, in the midst of his distress, triumphantly proclaimed his personal faith in a life after death. He looks forward to the end times and says,

> *I know that my Redeemer lives, and that in the end he will stand upon the earth. And after my skin has been destroyed, yet in my flesh I will see God; I myself will see him with my own eyes—I, and not another. How my heart yearns within me!* (Job 19:25-27).

Job likely expressed the hope of many Jews even though we read little of it in the pages of the Old Testament. Walvood notes, "Though the fact that all people who die will be raised is commonly assumed in the Old Testament, there are relatively few references that speak specifically of their resurrection."[30]

But, God spoke through the prophets and has given us an understanding that we can indeed expect a resurrection of Jews, just as there will be a general resurrection of all persons, some to a reward and some to an everlasting punishment. Daniel spells out what may be the single Old Testament reference to everlasting life:

> *There will be a time of distress such as has not happened from the beginning of nations until then. But at that time your people—everyone whose name is found written in the book—will be delivered. Multitudes who sleep in the dust of the earth will awake: some to everlasting life, others to shame and everlasting contempt* (Daniel 12:1f).

We find support for a resurrection belief in Isaiah as well, "But your dead will live; their bodies will rise" (Isaiah 26:19). In Ezekiel's vision of the valley of dry bones, we find God being quite explicit in proclaiming a resurrection:

> *Therefore prophesy and say to them: 'This is what the Sovereign Lord says: O my people, I am going to open your graves and bring you up from them; I will bring you back to the land of Israel. Then you, my people, will know that I am the Lord, when I open your graves and bring you up from them'* (Ezekiel 37:12f).

From these passages we find several important aspects of the Jew's resurrection. From Daniel, we discover the timing of it. He describes the Great Tribulation and indicates that it is then that the righteous ones will be raised. Daniel also was instructed to write that there would be two parts of the Jewish resurrection. The righteous would be part of the first resurrection. The unrighteous would not be raised until after the one thousand year reign of Christ to face judgment at the Great White Throne along with all others who have rejected God's offer of grace and pardon.

The message from God through Ezekiel indicates that no matter where the Jewish faithful were when raised from the dead, they would be taken back to the land of Israel. Thus, they would be in place to take their responsibilities of service in the Messiah's Kingdom.

Jesus Himself confirmed this essential truth. When the Jews were persecuting Him, as recorded in John 5, He gave them a quick lesson in who He was and what God was doing through Him. He included this key thought: "I tell you the truth, a time is coming and has now come when the dead will hear the voice of the Son of God and those who hear will live" (John 5:25).

At the return of Jesus when He comes from heaven accompanied by His Bride, He will add to His retinue not only the Jewish remnant who will come to Him to be saved, but the resurrected saints of the Old Testament will be gathered to Him as well. What a day it will be!

No. 14: Reigning With Messiah in His Kingdom

After the remnant of the Jews surviving the Tribulation have come to faith in Yeshua as Messiah and have been reunited with the Old Testament saints who have been resurrected, what comes next for the Jews? Here is where it gets really interesting! To really understand what is going to take place in the end, we really need to go back to the beginning. For it was God Himself who said, "I make known the end from the beginning" (Isaiah 46:10).

What Scripture could most likely help us to know what we can expect after the return of Jesus in power and glory? What could fill in the blanks for us in understanding the reign of Messiah on the earth for 1,000 years? Many persons miss the fact that after His return, Jesus is going to be reigning here on earth. Gerry Woltman reminds us, "However, when all is said and done, humans make the transition from This Present Age to the Millennial Age as earthlings on the planet Earth."[31]

To grasp the great significance of this end of the age experience for the Jews, we must return to the covenant which God made with these people through Abraham. What He promised in the beginning will be what we will see in the conclusion.

> *"I will make you into a great nation and I will bless you; I will make your name great and you will be a bless-ing. I will bless those who bless you, and whoever curses you I will curse; and all peoples on earth will be blessed through you"* (Genesis 12:2f).

There we have what God said in the beginning. And we can expect God to make this come to pass in the end as well. While all of these promises have been reality to some extent and at various times for the Jews, they have never been totally and fully in evidence on a permanent basis. That will change! When the Messiah is on the throne, the Jews will be seeing God's blessings coming to them in a new and abundant fashion. Ice and Price summarize this period well:

> *Upon His return to earth, Christ will set up His King-dom in Jerusalem (Isaiah 2:3,4; Zechariah 14:9) with Is-*

215

rael as the head of the nations of the world (Isaiah 2:2; Zechariah 8:21-23). He will rule the entire earth for a thousand years. In Jewish theology this is called the Days of Messiah., a golden age of spiritual life predicted by the prophets in which Israel fulfills its divine purpose as the "servant of the Lord" by being a light to the nations.[32]

The difference is that previously the Jews have only been beneficiaries of God's blessing spasmodically as their spiritual relationship to Him has been terribly inconsistent. When they come to Him in faith and become partakers of the New Covenant in Christ, they will at last be ready to be blessed and to be a blessing. The Kingdom ruled over by Messiah will insure that all nations and people will bless Israel and in return they will be blessed. So God's plan for the Jews as spelled out in the beginning will be what we should prepare to see in the Millennial age.

While specific duties during the 1,000 years are not clearly defined in Scripture, there does seem to be the sense that Israel will find itself in a role above that of other nations. Isaiah 61:5-6 would appear to indicate this as true. There it says that strangers and foreigners will be doing the agricultural work and Israel would be enjoying the wealth of the nations. God says to Israel, "But you will be called the priests of the Lord; you will be spoken of as ministers of our God."

Thus, it appears that a major responsibility of the Jews will be to insure the spiritual worship and service of God. We of the Gentile Church (strangers and foreigners) will likely discover that we may have leadership in the more mundane aspects of life in the Kingdom. Hal Lindsey addresses this:

The fact remains that all Old Testament prophecies about Gentiles picture them in a subordinate role to the Jew in the Messianic kingdom. There is some justification for the old rabbinical teaching of Jewish supremacy in the Millennial Kingdom.[33]

In the final analysis, however, it makes little difference who is doing what because it is the kingdom of our God and of His Christ, not the kingdom of men. Whatever tasks anyone has there will be a joyous act of serving the King. God gave Daniel the ability to interpret King Nebuchadnezzar's dream about nations in the end time. The capstone of that analysis was that all the kingdoms would come to naught as they were destroyed as "a rock was cut out, but not by human hands. It struck the statue on its feet of iron and clay and smashed them." The statue was a symbol of the kingdoms of this world. Daniel goes on to report that "the rock that struck the statue became a huge mountain and filled the whole earth" (Daniel 2:34,35).

To make sure that the meaning was not missed, God had Daniel prophesy further, "In the time of those kings, the God of Heaven will set up a kingdom that will never be destroyed, nor will it be left to another people. It will crush all those kingdoms and bring them to an end, but it will itself endure forever" (Daniel 2:44). Elwood McQuaid has a most exciting analysis of what those days during the reign of King Jesus will be like for the Jews.

After centuries of dispersion and unwarranted vilification, followed by decades of an agonizing search for peace, at long last true peace will come—the kind that the Jewish people have longed for over the centuries and the millennia. They will no longer be regarded as a pariah among he nations. Rather, Israel will be regarded as a partner whom the nations of the world will be happy to join in building up the walls of Jerusalem and the cities of the Promised Land.[34]

The Kingdom in which the Jews will participate will be a new Kingdom which will dominate all the other nations. Froese has stated well the dramatic outcome which the world can expect: "The entire global system, which includes more than 200 countries, has no future, but the kingdom God has established shall stand forever!"[35]

No. 15: Regain Position of Being a Blessing

This final topic of what's ahead for the Jews is closely related to the previous one. There are two major facets to the promise which God gave: the Jews would be blessed and they would be a blessing. To be in their own land and sharing in the development and operation of the kingdom of the Messiah will certainly a blessing to the Jews. But the experience of being a blessing is another matter. The two are always closely linked together. It is nearly impossible to be used of God as a blessing to others unless we are in a spiritual position in which we are first blessed by God.

What can we expect to see of blessings flowing through and from the Jews to the other nations? There will certainly be many. Just to be living in a world where righteousness, justice and holiness prevails will indeed be a welcomed blessing. The opportunity for peace and prosperity will be the norm in that new Kingdom. Blessings in God's eyes may have a much deeper purpose, however.

218

God is expecting a spiritual blessing to be universally forth-coming in those days. After the Tribulation has ended and Israel has come to know Messiah, Daniel reports God's plan: "Those who are wise will shine like the brightness of the heavens, and those who lead many to righteousness, like the stars for ever and ever" (Daniel 12:3). This is the Lord's purpose for all who claim .to belong to Himself, that they lead many to righteousness. There will be great multitudes of persons born during the Millennium and all will need to be led to righteousness

Another prophet is given a similar vision of what will take place when the Kingdom of Messiah is functioning:

> *In the last days the mountain of the Lord's temple will be established as chief among the mountains; it will be raised above the hills, and all nations will stream to it. Many people will come and say, "Come let us go up to the mountain of the Lord of the God of Jacob. He will teach us his ways, so that we may walk in his paths." The law of the Lord will go out from Zion, the word of the Lord from Jerusalem* (Isaiah 12:2f).

Indeed, the nations and people of the world have already been richly blessed by the Jewish people, although they have largely received animosity in return. The world has been greatly enriched by the inventive, financial and technological genius of the Jews. They have given us the Old Testament with a system of laws that form the basis for all the laws that civilized nations use to regulate society. The New Testament account of the birth and growth of Christianity was the work almost exclusively of Hebrews who had come to know Jesus as Messiah. And, of course, the greatest blessing of all is that of a Jewish Messiah offering salvation to the entire world.

However, the fullest blessings which God wants to bestow through the Jews are still ahead of us and will only be realized when Israel will be walking in fellowship with their Messiah in His earthly Kingdom and are available to Him to bless all the other peoples of the earth. My friend and prophecy teacher Gary Fisher has succinctly written of that coming time:

> *Israel will finally become what she was called out and separated to do, be the world's teacher in what it means to know the Lord and His righteousness. After so many centuries of enduring the world's hatred and disrespect, how many of us long to see Israel rise to this glorious time of respect and admiration from the world. Israel's Messiah, Jesus, will lead the world into the greatest time of peace and righteousness ever known on earth.*[36]

There are peoples and groups today, such as Iran, Hamas, Hezbollah and ISIS, whose express purpose is to annihilate the Jews forever. They know not the Word of God nor the plan of God for His people, the Jews. If they did, they would realize their goals are doomed for failure. God isn't finished with the Jews. He has great plans which He told from the beginning to bless them and through them to bless the rest of the world. The greatest days for the Jewish people are ahead, and it may not be long until all these things come to pass.

$$\text{❄} \quad \text{❄} \quad \text{❄}$$

This study has become far longer than I ever envisioned when I set out to write it. It was not originally planned as a part of this book. But the Lord gave me the direction one sleepless night that it should be included. The next morning I began to set down the major items that I understand the Bible tells us are ahead for the Jewish people. Quickly the list grew to fifteen. I have endeavored to keep the sections as sketchy as possible, but found that even writing the minimum turned out to be saying a lot.

The good thing is that the quantity of this chapter may be a good reminder of the vast number of things which are still ahead for the Jews. As I have written, the Lord has given me not only a more thorough knowledge of God's plan, but also a deeper appreciation and love for these people of God, however faulty their example of faith may be. For they provide the root and foundation of all I believe about our Heavenly Father and His Son and my Savior Jesus.

John Walvoord has been among the leading students and teachers of Bible prophecy. I appreciate his summary of what is taking place among the Jewish people today and how it must stir us to readiness for the End-Time rushing in upon us.

The study of the history and prophecy of Israel is not a mere academic exercise on the part of the theologian or Bible student, but provides an unparalleled perspective of the majestic dealings of God with this prophetic nation. In it is revealed the faithfulness of God to the people whom He sovereignly chose, the effective outworking of God's wise purpose for them in spite of failure, delay, and indifference to God's will. The fact that in our day there is again movement and development in relation to this ancient nation is a sign that the stage is being set for the final world drama. Certainly as Israel's promises are being fulfilled before our eyes, other aspects of prophecy such as the resurrection of the dead in Christ and the translation of living saints become a real and imminent possibility. The hope of Israel is also the hope of the church.[37]

So we conclude this fascinating study of the future. I plead with you to allow the Lord to give you a greater love and understanding for Israel and the Jewish people. I leave you with a final exhortation which is not mine but that of King David found in Psalm 122:6. *"Sha'alu Shalom Yerushalayim*—Pray for the Peace of Jerusalem."

Study Seven Notes

1. John Hagee, *From Daniel to Doomsday*, Thomas Nelson Publishers, Nashville, © 1999, p. 3.
2. Wikipedia contributors, "Theodor Herzl," *Wikipedia, The Free Encyclopedia*, (accessed May 28, 2014).
3. Elwood McQuaid, *The Zion Connection*, Harvest House, Eugene, OR, © 1996, p. 78f.
4. John F. Walvoord, *Israel in Prophecy*, Zondervan Publishing House, Grand Rapids, MI, © 1962, p. 47f.
5. Mike Evans, *Jerusalem Betrayed*, Word Publishing, Dallas, TX, © 1997, p. 189.
6. Perry Stone, *Living in the Final Chapter*, Voice of Evangelism, Cleveland, TN, © 2008, p. 16f.
7. Michael D. Evans, *Beyond Iraq*, White Stone Books, Lakeland, FL, © 2003, p. 94.
8. Wendy Beckett, *God Keeps Covenant*, © 2006, p. 28.
9. John F. Walvoord, *Major Bible Prophecies*, Harper Paperbacks, New York, NY, © 1991, p. 97.
10. Randall Price, *The Battle for the Last Days Temple*, Harvest House Publishers, Eugene, OR, © 2004, p. 73.
11. Mike Evans, op.cit., p. 193
12. Dore Gold, *The Fight for Jerusalem*, Regnery Publishing, Inc., Washington, DC, © 2007, p. 119.
13. Mike Evans, op.cit., p. 96.
14. Hal Lindsey, *Planet Earth*, Western Front, Ltd., Beverly Hills, CA, © 1998, p. 64.
15. Thomas S. McCall & Zola Levitt, *Coming the End!*, Zola Levitt Ministries, Dallas, TX, © 1999, p. 63.

16. Ibid., p. 109f.
17. Arno Froese, *Daniel's Prophecies Made Easy*, Midnight Call Ministries, Columbia, SC, © 2004, p. 184.
18. Mark Hitchcock, *Could the Rapture Happen Today?*, Multnomah Publishers, Sisters, OR, © 2005, p. 114.
19. John Hagee, Editor, *Prophecy Study Bible*, Thomas Nelson Publishers, Nashville, TN, © 1997, p.1002.
20. Randall Price, op.cit., p. 58.
21. Thomas Ice & Randall Price, *Ready to Rebuild*, Harvest House Publishers, Eugene, OR, © 1992, p. 49f.
22. John Hagee, *From Daniel to Doomsday*, op. cit., p. 168.
23. Thomas Ice & Randall Price, op. cit., p. 231f.
24. Charles W. Carter, Editor, *The Wesleyan Bible Commentary*, Eerdmans Publishing Co., Grandd Rapids, MI, © 1965, p. 72.
25. John F. Walvoord, *Major Bible Prophecies*, op. cit., p. 449.
26. William G. Woltman, *The Hitchhiker's Guide to the Apocalypse*, Kingdom Projects, Avon Park, FL, © 2012, p. 7.
27. Thomas Ice & Randall Price, op. cit., p. 232.
28. Hall Lindsey, *Vanished Into Thin Air*, Western Front, Ltd., Minneapolis, MN, © 1999, p. 199.
29. Arno Froese, op. cit., p. 63.
30. Gary Fisher, *Israel in Bible Prophecy*, Lion of Judah Ministry, Franklin, TN, © 2007, p. 10.
31. John F. Walvoord, *Israel in Prophecy*, op. cit., p. 130.

Other Books on BIBLE PROPHECY by Ray Bachman

The Love Letters of Jesus reveals what Jesus will be expecting in His Bride when He returns as the Bridegroom in the Rapture to take her to be with Himself. A major emphasis is given to the letters Jesus sent to the seven churches of Asia as recorded in Revelation two and three. While it covers major prophetic subjects, it does so in an easy to understand manner. 312 pages, 5½" x 8½"
Order at: www.createspace.com/3392189
Also available from Amazon or author.

The God Who Remembers is a study guide to the Biblical prophet Zechariah. This sometimes difficult book is made simple for even newer prophecy students. There are fill-the-blank study sheets at the end of each chapter for review, group discussion or use for leader's presentation. The large format 8½" x 11" book of 148 pages makes an excellent small group study. Contact the author for church or group discount.

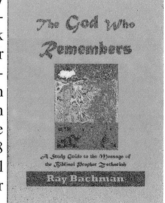

Order at: www.createspace.com/3708721
Also available from Amazon or author

The Study Guide

A companion resource to aid your study of this book

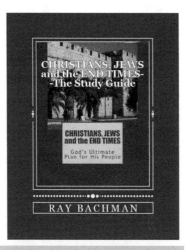

CHRISTIANS, JEWS and the END TIMES —The Study Guide

Are you a person who has one of those memories that so wonderfully grasp what you read? Are you able to quickly analyze and store in your mental file the content you are likely to need to recall? And are you able to do so without rereading the book? If so, you are likely not a prospect for this study guide.

However, most of the rest of us will find this guide a most helpful tool in enabling us to absorb what we are reading in *Christians, Jews and the End Times.* The fill-the-blank pages are multipurpose. They can be used to help grasp the outline as we read. They are dynamic as a self-test to see how well we grasped what we have just studied. They make an excellent discussion outline for use with friends or in a small group setting. Or they can be applied by a group leader as a lesson outline and filled in by the group as the class is conducted. However they are used, they will enrich your study of this very current and important topic.

AVAILAB LE LATE 2016
Online at: https:www.createspace.com/6318630 or Amazon
From author at: bachmanjr@gmail.com
Discount pricing for church or group study at bachmanjr@gmail.com